# CONNECTING TO THE QURAN

# CONNECTING TO THE QURAN

## Imam al-Nawawi's Abridged Guide to Practical Etiquette with the Quran

*Translation & notes by*

MUSA FURBER

Connecting to the Quran: Imam al-Nawawi's Abridged Guide to Practical Etiquette with the Quran



ISBN 978-1-944904-13-5 (paper)
978-1-944904-12-8 (EPUB)

Published by:
Islamosaic
islamosaic.com

بسم الله الرحمن الرحيم

All praise is to Allah alone, the Lord of the Worlds
And may He send His benedictions upon
our master Muhammad, his Kin
and his Companions
and grant them
peace

# *Transliteration Key*

ء ʾ (A distinctive glottal stop made at the bottom of the throat.)

ا ā, a

ب b

ت t

ث th (Pronounced like the *th* in *think*.)

ج j

ح ḥ (Hard *h* sound made at the Adam's apple in the middle of the throat.)

خ kh (Pronounced like *ch* in Scottish *loch*.)

د d

ذ dh (Pronounced like *th* in *this*.)

ر r (A slightly trilled *r* made behind the upper front teeth.)

ز z

س s

ش sh

ص ṣ (An emphatic *s* pronounced behind the upper front teeth.)

ض ḍ (An emphatic *d*-like sound made by pressing the entire tongue against the upper palate.)

ط ṭ (An emphatic *t* sound produced behind the front teeth.)

ظ ẓ (An emphatic *th* sound, like the *th* in *this*, made behind the front teeth.)

ع ʿ (A distinctive Semitic sound made in the middle of the throat and sounding to a Western ear more like a vowel than a consonant.)

غ gh (A guttural sound made at the top of the throat resembling the untrilled German and French *r*.)

ف f

ق q (A hard *k* sound produced at the back of the palate.)

ك k

ل l

م m

ن n

ه h (This sound is like the English *h* but has more body. It is made at the very bottom of the throat and pronounced at the beginning, middle, and ends of words.)

و ū, u

ي ī, i, y

ﷺ A supplication made after mention of the Prophet Muḥammad, translated as "May Allah bless him and give him peace."

# *Contents*

# *Preface*

In the Name of Allah, Most Merciful and Compassionate

I have taught my translation of Imam al-Nawawi's *Etiquette with the Quran* (*Al-Tibyan fi adab hamalet Al-Quran*) several times. With each lesson, I would add notes to my working PDF, with the goal of improving the accessibility of the text by distilling it down to its essential components. But despite a PDF filled with copious annotations, corrections, alternative phrases, and directives on which sections to skip and which ones to focus more attention upon, I am still left at the end of each reading wanting to simplify and shorten the book further. My intention is to make it even easier for students to read and benefit from the book's many lessons so that they may interact with the Quran in a proper manner, strengthen their connection to the Quran, increase the impact their recitation has on them and, God willing, raise their standing in the afterlife.

By Allah's generosity and mercy, I recently discovered that Imam al-Nawawi (may Allah grant him His mercy) abridged *Al-Tibyan*. While I knew that Imam al-Nawawi had included a decent portion of *Al-Tibyan* in *Al-Adkhar*, and that Imam al-Suyuti (may Allah grant him His mercy) included a meta-abridgment of *Al-Tibyan* and relevant material from Imam al-Nawawi's other works in *Al-Itqan fi 'ulum Al-Quran* (since I had relied on both books while editing the first edition of my translation), I was not aware that Imam al-Nawawi had produced his own abridgment as a separate book. Needless to say, I was thrilled about this turn of events and proceeded to work on a translation.

The bulk of the English text in this book comes from *Etiquette with the Quran*. But since I want something as simple as possible, I have removed nonessential transliteration characters and Arabic words, and have kept footnotes to a bare minimum. Throughout this book, the word "prayer" is used for the Arabic word "*salat*," which refers to the canonical prayer Muslims perform daily, and which opens with the saying of "*Allahu akbar*" and ends with "*As-salamu 'alaykum*." The word is capitalized when referring to a specific prayer, such as the Mid-Afternoon Prayer. "Supplication" is used in place of the Arabic word "*du'a*," and "litany" is a substitute for the Arabic "*dhikr*," which refers to a series of devotional phrases that Muslims utter in remembrance of Allah Most High.

And just as Imam al-Nawawi (may Allah grant him His mercy) advises readers interested in more details to look at his original work, I likewise encourage readers to explore my translation of that work.

Many thanks are owed to Khalid Gonçalves and his generous offer to edit the text. Every text he edits is markedly improved by his touch. Last but not least, I owe much to my wife and children for their constant support and sacrifice over the years. Please include these individuals in your supplications.

Where I have succeeded, it is only through the grace of Allah; where I have faltered, it is from my own shortcomings. May Allah forgive and bless Imam al-Nawawi, everyone mentioned in this book, its owners, readers, listeners, and all Muslims—living and dead. And may He make us worthy of being among the honored bearers of the Quran.

MUSA FURBER

KUALA LUMPUR

NOVEMBER 22, 2018

## *Biography of Imam al-Nawawi*

Yahya ibn Sharaf "Muhya al-Din" Abu Zakariyya al-Nawawi lived from 1233–1277 AH/631–676 AH. Imam al-Nawawi is named after his hometown of Nawa near Damascus. He is the pious, ascetic, most learned, scrupulously Godwary, accomplished jurist and hadith master, known as the impeccable "Shaykh al-Islam" by the unanimity of the people of the Sunnah of the Prophet (may Allah bless him and grant him peace). Imam al-Nawawi was fearless before kings, yet lordly and chaste. He died young yet, in his lifespan of forty-five years, produced unprecedented works of learning that elevated him to the status of principal authority in the later Shafi'i school. Imam al-Dhahabi (may Allah grant him His mercy) described him as "the standard-bearer of the Friends of Allah." Imam al-Nawawi himself said, "Allah has blessed me in the right use of my time," in reference to his own remarkable scholarly output and achievements.

Imam al-Sakhawi (may Allah grant him His mercy) described al-Nawawi as "the spiritual pole of the noble Friends of Allah, the legist of humankind, the reviver of the Sunnah, and the slayer of innovation." May Allah bestow great and endless mercy on him, bless him, and reward him on behalf of every Muslim!

### *Early Education and Teachers*

Imam al-Nawawi came to Damascus in 649 AH. In four and a half months, he memorized Abu Ishaq al-Shirazi's manual of Shafi'i fiqh entitled *Al-Tanbih* (may Allah grant him His mercy) and a quarter of *Al-Muhadhdhab fi al-Madhhab*, after which he went on the Pilgrimage with his father—ailing during most of the trip—and took up residence in Medina for a month and a half before finally returning to Damascus.

Regarding his early studies, the Imam said, "It occurred to me to study medicine, so I bought the *Qanun* of Ibn Sina (may Allah grant him His mercy), whereupon darkness filled my heart and I remained unable to work for several days. Then I came to my senses and sold the *Qanun*, after which light filled my heart." Shaykh 'Abd al-Fattah Abu Ghudda (may Allah grant him His mercy) commented: "In this way does Allah Most High create in souls attraction for one type of knowledge and aversion to another, proficiency in one, and deficiency in another; and in this there are great examples of wisdom, both hidden and manifest."[1]

While in his period of intensive study, the Imam said there were six years during which he wasted absolutely no time, whether day or night: he was completely devoted to his studies, even when walking in the street. And it was only after this period that he began writing and teaching.

---

1. 'Abd al-Fattāḥ Abū Ghudda, *Al-'Ulamā' al-'Uzzāb*, p. 147.

***His Asceticism and Humble Way of Life***

Imam al-Nawawi was a strict ascetic in the manner of the early Muslims, neither eating nor sleeping except out of necessity. He fasted continually throughout the year, eating a simple dish at nightfall and drinking some water before dawn. This he did once every twenty-four hours. He avoided moist foods, such as fruits and cucumber, in order not to induce drowsiness. He dressed austerely, owning only one long shirt and a small turban. He divided his time between worship and learning.

***His Superlative Mastery of Hadith and Jurisprudence***

In addition to his perseverance in the struggle against the ego, his application of scrupulous Godfearingness, watchfulness, and discipline over his soul (and purification from its defects), he was also a master of hadith and its sciences, and a foremost authority in the [Shafi'i] school. Imam al-Nawawi's verdicts on narrator-commendation are generally identical to those of Imam Ibn Hajar al-'Asqalani (may Allah grant him His mercy), which is a remarkable assessment in view of Ibn Hajar's position as the greatest of all hadith masters after the luminaries of the early centuries.

***His Fearless Admonishing of Princes***

Imam al-Nawawi would address those in power and admonish them for the sake of Allah, in accordance with the obligation of "admonishing princes" which he himself defined as "admonishing the leaders of the Muslims consists of... appraising them of any remiss of which they are unaware concerning the rights of Muslims." He did this several times in the palace of al-Malik al-Zahir (may Allah grant him His mercy) who once exclaimed, "I am frightened of him!"

### *Headmastership of Dar Al-Hadith Al-Ashrafiyya in Damascus*

He took up the headmastership of Dar al-Hadith al-Ashrafiyya in Damascus after the death of his Shaykh Abu Shama (may Allah grant him His mercy) in 665 AH and held it until his own death eleven years later, never accepting any compensation for his needs.

In the time of Imam al-Nawawi, Dar al-Hadith had the noble sandal of the Prophet (Allah bless him and give him peace) in its possession. The sandal was kept in a wooden box above the *mihrab* (prayer niche) in its mosque. The mosque, however, was burnt by the Tatars and the relic disappeared, but the *mihrab* remains intact, in the mosque of Dar al-Hadith's preparatory school, near the Umawi Mosque in Damascus.

### *Select Bibliography of Shaykh al-Islam*

In his brief but blessed life, Imam al-Nawawi authored nearly fifty books. These volumes are—like their author—among the treasures of Islam and contain an immense blessing (*barakah*) bestowed by Allah. They are characterized by great diligence and scholarship. They are among the most relied-upon works of Islamic law and hadith in Islam. Some of them are listed below:

*Al-Arba'una hadith* (*The Forty Hadiths*) is the most widely read collection of its kind, in which the Imam chose forty of the most important hadiths that pertain to the spiritual and social life of the Muslims. It is a mark of divine approval of Imam al-Nawawi that Allah Most High has made him famous through this small booklet, as the *Arba'un* has been blessed for seven hundred years with unreserved approval and acceptance among Muslims worldwide.

*Riyad al-salihin* (*Garden of the Righteous*), which is one of the most widely read anthologies of prophetic traditions focusing on personal ethics. It is composed of three hundred and seventy-two chapters spread over nineteen books, with each chapter citing the *ayahs* of Quran and authentic hadiths that pertain to the subject at hand. The Imam finished compiling the work in mid-Ramadan of 670 AH.

*Al-Adhkar al-muntakhaba min kalam sayyid al-abrar* (*Supplications Chosen from the Discourse of the Master of the Pious*) is the quintessential treatise of its kind, unmatched by any other. It contains three hundred and forty-nine chapters and addresses every situation Muslims face in their private and public lives, adducing the appropriate supplication for each as related from the Prophet (Allah bless him and give him peace), with sound, fair, or weak chains of transmission. Imam Ibn Hajar al-'Asqalani taught six hundred and sixty classes devoted to the documentation of the *Adhkar*, some of which were recently published in three volumes. Imam Ibn 'Allan al-Ṣiddiqi (may Allah grant him His mercy) wrote a nine-volume commentary on the *Adhkar,* titled *Al-Futuhat al-rabbaniyya 'ala Al-Adhkar al-Nawawiyya.*

*Sharh Sahih Muslim* ranks among the great masterpieces of Islamic literature. The Imam titled it *Al-Minhaj fi sharh Sahih Muslim ibn al-Hajjaj* (*The Method: A Commentary on Sahih Muslim ibn al-Hajjaj*). The work is built upon previous works by the Maliki scholars al-Qadi 'Iyad and al-Mazari (may Allah grant them His mercy). It numbers about twenty volumes in print.

*Wird al-Imam al-Nawawi* is the Imam's daily devotional supplications and invocations.

*Al-Majma' sharh Al-Muhadhdhab* (*The Compendium: Commentary of the Muhadhdhab*) is Al-Nawawi's unfinished magnum opus of Shafi'i fiqh.

*Rawdat al-talibin* (*The Seeker's Garden*), a medium-sized reference manual in Shafi'i fiqh, and the smaller *Minhaj al-talibin* (*The Seeker's Road*) are, respectively, abridgments of *Sharh Al-Wajiz* (also known as *Al-Sharh al-kabir*) and *Al-Muharrar*—both by Imam al-Raf'i' (may Allah grant him His mercy).

### Imam al-Nawawi's Death

Returning to Nawa from a trip to Jerusalem and Hebron, the Imam and Friend of Allah died in his father's house after a short illness.

(This biography is based on work by G. F. Haddad. See *Etiquette with the Quran* for more details.)

# *Author's Introduction*

In the Name of Allah, Most Merciful and Compassionate

Praise be to Allah, the Benefactor, Possessor of Infinite Power, Superiority, and Perfection, who guided us to belief and who has made our religion superior to all the rest. He graced us by sending us the one most noble unto Him, Muhammad (may Allah bless him and grant him peace), through whom He effaced idol-worship. He honored him with the miraculous Quran, which endures despite the passing of time. With it, He challenges humankind and jinn in their entirety; and with it, He silences the misguiders and transgressors. He made it a comfort for the hearts of the insightful and the perceptive. It does not become dulled with frequent repetition and the changing of time. He has made it easy to remember so that even young children may memorize it. He multiplied the reward for reciting it, and extolled it greatly.

I offer Him the greatest praise for this and for the innumerable graces He has bestowed upon us in all times and occasions. I ask Him for the generous bestowal of [His] good favor upon me and all of my loved ones. I testify that there is no deity other than Allah, a testimony which attains forgiveness, saves from the Fire anyone who utters it, and brings one to reside in Paradise.

To commence, Allah Sublime and Most High has graced this nation (may He increase it and its people in honor) with the religion that He has chosen for Himself: the religion of Islam. He has graced us by sending the best of His creation: Muhammad—may the most eminent of blessings, bounties, and peace be conferred upon him. And He honored us with His Book, the best of all speech. Allah Sublime and Most High gathered in it all that is needed; it includes stories of the first people and the last, spiritual counsel, similitudes, etiquette, and rulings of all types. And it includes clear, unshakable proofs indicating His absolute unity, and other things that His messengers (may Allah bless them and give them peace) brought: irrefutable arguments against the followers of ignoble heresies. He encourages us to recite it; He orders us to heed it and give it veneration, to adhere to it through proper conduct, and to spend generously in honoring it.

I have seen [the people of our land, Damascus (may Allah Most High protect and preserve it, and all other lands of Islam),] concentrating on reciting the Mighty Quran through studying, instructing, reading, and learning it—in groups and individually. They spend enormous effort in this, day and night (may Allah increase their desire for it and for all kinds of obedience), desiring thereby the pleasure of Allah, the Possessor of Majesty and Honor.

This inspired me to put together a concise treatise concerning the proper etiquette to be observed by the bearers of the Quran, and the characteristics of its memorizers and students.

I compiled this, clarified it, explained it, and did it skillfully. I named it *Al-Tibyan fi adab hamalat al-Qur'an* [published as "*Etiquette with the Quran*"]. Within it, I mentioned precious matters that memorizers [of the Quran] must know; and it would be repugnant and frustrating for them to remain ignorant of these matters. I then saw that it would be good to abridge my treatise to facilitate its memorization and dissemination. So I began this endeavor with the goal of greatly condensing it while retaining clarity of expression, hinting at some of its evidences, and [mentioning] rulings that can be understood via allusion. Anyone who has questions about anything mentioned herein and desires more information should seek it in *Al-Tibyan,* for there—if Allah wills—he will find its rulings and pronunciation clearly laid out. Reliance is upon Allah the Generous. I resign my affairs to Him and lean upon Him. Allah is my reliance and the best of agents.

Its contents are the following:

1. The merit of reciting and bearing the Quran
2. The precedence of recitation and of reciters
3. Honoring the folk of the Quran
4. The etiquette of its teachers and students
5. The etiquette of its bearers
6. The etiquette of recitation (which is the bulk of the book and its main goal)
7. The etiquette of all people with the Quran

8. Verses and chapters recommended at particular times
9. Writing the Quran and respecting its written form

# 1

# *The Merit of Reciting & Bearing the Quran*

Allah Mighty and Majestic says, "Those who read the Book of Allah, and establish prayer, and spend, secretly and openly, from that which He has bestowed on them, they look forward to imperishable gain, so that He will fully recompense them their wages and increase them of His grace," (Quran, 35:29–30).

'Uthman ibn 'Affan (may Allah be pleased with him) said that the Messenger of Allah (may Allah bless him and grant him peace) said, "The best among you is one who learns the Quran and teaches it." (Bukhari; Muslim)

'A'ishah (may Allah be pleased with her) said that the Messenger of Allah (may Allah bless him and grant him peace) said, "The one who recites the Quran stammering, it being difficult for him, has two rewards." (Bukhari; Muslim)

Ibn 'Umar (may Allah be pleased with them both) stated that the Prophet (may Allah bless him and grant him peace) said, "There is no envy except concerning two: a person to whom Allah has given the Quran and he conforms to it night and day; and a person to whom Allah has given wealth, from which he spends [charitably] night and day." (Bukhari; Muslim)

'Abdallah ibn Mas'ud (may Allah be pleased with him) also transmitted the hadith, but with the following wording: "There is no envy except concerning two: a person to whom Allah has given wealth and he expended it all for the sake of Allah, and a person to whom Allah has given wisdom and he judges according to it and teaches it." (Bukhari; Muslim)

Abu Umama al-Bahili (may Allah be pleased with him) reported that the Messenger of Allah (may Allah bless him and grant him peace) said, "Recite the Quran, for on the Day of Judgment, it will come to intercede for its companion." (Muslim)

'Umar ibn al-Khattab (may Allah be pleased with him) stated that the Prophet (may Allah bless him and grant him peace) said, "Allah Most High exalts some groups with this Book, and debases others." (Muslim)

Ibn 'Abbas (may Allah be well pleased with him and his father) stated that the Messenger of Allah (may Allah bless him and grant him peace) said, "Someone without Quran in his heart is like a ruined house." (Tirmidhi: a well-rigorously authenticated hadith)

## 2

# *The Precedence of Recitation & of Reciters*

The Messenger of Allah (may Allah bless him and grant him peace) said, "Whosoever is the best in reciting the Book of Allah Most High should lead the people [in prayer]." (Muslim)

Ibn Abbas (may Allah be pleased with him) said, "The reciters were the companions of the assembly of 'Umar (may Allah be pleased with him) and his council, whether middle-aged or young." (Bukhari)

As the Prophet (may Allah bless him and grant him peace) was burying the martyrs from the Battle of Uhud, he (may Allah bless him and grant him peace) ordered that the one who was best at reciting the Quran be placed closest to the direction of prayer [*qibla*]." (Muslim)

Know that the soundest position—the one followed by the scholars who are relied upon—is that reciting the Quran is superior to all other forms of remembrance. The evidence for this is patently obvious.

# 3

## *Honoring the Folk of the Quran*

Allah Most High says, "And he who reveres the rites of Allah, it is from Godfearingness in the heart" (Quran, 22:32); "He who reveres what Allah has deemed sacred, that is better for him with his Lord" (Quran, 22:30); "And those who malign believing men and believing women undeservedly, they bear the guilt of slander and manifest sin," (Quran, 33:58).

This chapter includes the hadiths mentioned in the previous chapter.

Abu Musa al-Ash'ari (may Allah be pleased with him) stated that the Prophet (may Allah bless him and grant him peace) said, "Exalting Allah Most High includes giving honor to the gray-haired Muslim, to whomever bears the Quran without exceeding its proper bounds or shunning it, and to any person of authority who acts justly." (Abu Dawud: a well-authenticated hadith.)

The Prophet (may Allah bless him and grant him peace) related that Allah Mighty and Majestic said, "Whoever shows enmity to a friend of mine, I have declared war upon [him]." (Bukhari)

The two venerable shaykhs, Abu Hanifa and al-Shafi'i (may Allah Most High have mercy upon them both) said, "If the scholars are not the Friends [*awliya'*] of Allah, then Allah has no friends."

# 4

# *The Etiquette of Teachers & Students of the Quran*

Teachers and students should both engage in the recitation [of the Quran] for the purpose of gaining the pleasure of Allah Most High. Allah Most High says, "And they were ordered no more than to worship Allah sincerely, keeping religion pure for Him, being upright, to establish the prayer, and to give obligatory charity. And that is the worthy religion," (Quran, 98:5).

'Umar (may Allah be pleased with him) related that the Messenger of Allah (may Allah bless him and grant him peace) said, "Actions are only [valued] according to their intentions, and each person has only what he has intended." (Bukhari; Muslim)

Ibn 'Abbas (may Allah be pleased with them both) said, "A man memorizes to the degree of his intention."

The sages said, "Sincerity is purifying the action from being observed by people." And they said, "Sincerity is the worshiper's actions being identical in what is manifest and what is hidden."

***Not Seeking a Worldly Objective***

One's studies and teaching must not be for the purpose of attaining some worldly objective, such as wealth, leadership, influence, status above one's peers, gaining people's praise, or drawing others' attention to oneself. Allah Most High says, "Whoever desires the immediate [gains of this world], We hasten what We will to whomever We will," (Quran, 17:18).

A Quran instructor does not dishonor his teaching by hoping to obtain some favor—by way of an [influential] student who recites to him—whether the favor is in the form of property or some service, however small, or even a gift that he would not have received had it not been for [his] student reciting to him.

The teacher takes every precaution to refrain from boasting because of the many people under his tutelage and who patronize him. He is cautious about disliking his students reciting with someone else who offers them benefit. These afflictions put some ignorant teachers to the test, and they are clear indications of the evil intention and corrupt innermost mettle of whoever possesses them. Indeed, they are sure proof of [the teacher's] lack of desire to teach for the sake of the noble pleasure of Allah Most High.

'Ali (may Allah be pleased with him) said, "O bearers of knowledge! Act according to [your knowledge], since the scholar is the one who acts according to what he has learned and whose knowledge corresponds to his action. There will be groups who possess knowledge that does not go beyond their collar bones. Their action contradicts their knowledge; their inward state contradicts their outward. They sit in circles vying with one another until a man becomes angry with the one he sits with, so he sits with someone else, leaving the other behind. Their actions in these assemblies of theirs do not ascend to Allah Most High." (*Musnad al-Darimi*)

### *Molded by Good Qualities*

The teacher should be molded by the good qualities mentioned in the Revelation, and the praiseworthy inner qualities and pleasing habits that Allah Most High calls attention to.

They include abstinence in this world, thinking little of it, and lacking concern for it and its worldly people. They also include generosity, openhandedness, noble character, a cheerful face, discernment, and self-control. They include avoiding vile forms of income, adhering to scrupulousness, humility, tranquility, dignity, modesty, submission, and avoiding laughter and frequent play. They also include adhering to religious tasks such as maintaining cleanliness and removing filth and hair that the Sacred Law mentions removing; trimming the mustache and nails and combing the beard; and removing offensive smells and offensive clothing.

The teacher should be perpetually conscious of Allah Most High, whether alone or in public.

### *Uprooting Sicknesses of the Heart*

He must take every precaution from the sicknesses of the heart, such as envy, pride, showing off, and thinking little of others—even if [they are] beneath him. He must not see himself as better than anyone else.

***Being Kind and Accommodating***

The teacher should be kind to whomever recites to him, welcoming him and being well-mannered with him in accordance to his circumstances.

He should make every effort to be sincere with whomever recites to him, given that sincere advice to others is obligatory, and they [his students] are even more worthy of it.

The teacher should not be arrogant towards his students.

The teacher must be openhanded by teaching students gently, being kind towards them, encouraging them to learn, and harmonizing their hearts.

He teaches them that the scholars are the inheritors of the Prophets (may Allah bless them and give them peace).

He his mindful of his student's well-being, just as he is mindful of his own and his son's. The teacher assumes the role of the student's father by having compassion for him, concern for his well-being, and patience with his roughness and ill manners. He even pardons his student's poor behavior in some circumstances. The teacher gently admonishes him about the ugliness of those acts so that he not repeat them. The teacher—without exception—should like for [his student] what he likes for himself, and dislike for him the shortcomings he dislikes in himself.

***Teaching the Merits of Knowledge and Manners***

The teacher should mention the superiority of learning to the student, so that it causes him to be eager and increases his desire, making him abstinent from this world and desirous of the afterlife.

The teacher should be fully committed to teaching [his students], preferring it over his personal worldly matters that are not critical. It is recommended that he empty his heart of all preoccupying matters—and there are many known to us—while sitting for their recitation. It is recommended that he be resolved to making his students understand.

He should give each student what is suitable for him. That is, he should not give a greater [workload] to one who cannot bear the increase, nor should he lessen the load for one who can indeed bear the addition.

The teacher should gradually discipline the student so that he may have excellent manners and a pleasant disposition; that he struggle against his lower self [*nafs*] by applying subtle tactics. The teacher should habituate him so as to safeguard all of his student's affairs, both private and public. The teacher should urge him repeatedly—in words and in deeds—to have sincerity, be truthful, have perfect intentions, and to be vigilant of Allah Most High at all times.

The teacher should inform him that through all of this, the light of spiritual knowledge will open to him, and his heart will also be opened; and the wellsprings of wisdom and subtleties will gush forth from his heart and Allah will bless him in his work and state of being, giving him success in whatever he says and does.

***Class Etiquette***

He should ask the students to repeat what they have memorized. Moreover, he should praise a student whose excellence is manifest, as long as there is no danger of conceit or something else that may be feared of him. He should gently admonish whoever falls short in his studies, as long as he does not fear alienating him.

When there are many students, the teacher gives precedence in instructing [his students] according to the order in which they arrive. He does not allow one who came earlier to give his spot to someone without a religious justification, since it is offensive to give others preferences in devotional matters.

He must check up on them, and ask about whomever is absent.

He does not deny anyone instruction because of unsound intentions. Sufyan [al-Thawri] and others said, "Their seeking knowledge is intention in itself." (And may Allah be pleased with them and grant them His mercy.)

***Not Fidgeting during Recitation***

During his student's recitation, the teacher should not fidget with his hands. He should keep his eyes from needlessly glancing about without a legal need, and he should not listen attentively except to the reciter. He should be in a state of ritual purity and seated facing the direction of prayer. And he sits in a dignified manner, wearing clothing that is white and clean.

When he reaches the place where he is to sit [to

teach], he prays two prayer-cycles [*rak'as*] before actually sitting, whether or not the location is a mosque. This practice is emphasized more if it is in a mosque, since it is offensive to sit in a mosque before praying. Also, he may sit cross-legged. It is related that 'Abdallah ibn Mas'ud (may Allah be pleased with him) would have people recite to him in the mosque while kneeling.

It is an emphasized etiquette that the teacher not disgrace the status of knowledge by teaching in a place associated with his student—whether the student is the caliph or a person of lower rank. Instead, he safeguards the knowledge from this, just as the Righteous Forebearers [*Salaf*] did (may Allah be pleased with them and grant them His mercy).

### *The Communal Obligation of Teaching*

Teaching is a communal obligation. If only one individual is qualified, it becomes his personal obligation. But in the context of a community, in which there is a group of people through whom [the duty of education] may be discharged and they fulfill it, the sin falls from the rest. If they refuse to teach, they all sin unless they have a legal excuse.

### *The Student's Etiquette*

All of the teacher's etiquette that we have mentioned is, in essence, the student's etiquette as well. But the student's etiquette also includes avoiding any concerns that preoccupy him from achieving [his objectives], except that which is unavoidable because of need. He should purify his heart from any corruption, so that it is fit for receiving the Quran, memorizing it, and profiting from it.

The student should show humility towards the knowledge, so that he attains it by means of his humility. Some have said in verse:

> Knowledge destroys the arrogant youth,
> like the torrent erodes high
> ground."

The student shows humility towards his [teacher's] knowledge and his person—even if he is younger, less famous, of a lower pedigree, less righteous, or lacking in other qualities.

The student should obey his teacher, consult him in his affairs, and accept his opinion. An ill person who is rational accepts the opinion of an experienced and sincere physician. [With religious knowledge,] this is even more appropriate.

***Studying with the Elite***

The student does not take knowledge except from someone whose competence is complete, his religiosity visible, has realized profound knowledge of Allah, and is well known as a person who is free of [debilitating] problems. The Righteous Forebearers (may Allah be pleased with them and grant them His mercy) have said, "This knowledge is religion, so examine well the one from whom you take your religion."

The student should look to his teacher with the eye

of respect, believing with unwavering conviction in his competence and superiority over his contemporaries.

The student visits his shaykh [with] most excellent manners, keeping himself tidy with everything we have just mentioned concerning the teacher: cleanliness, regular use of the toothstick, and a heart free of preoccupation. He does not enter without seeking permission, unless the teacher is in a place that does not require it.

The student greets the attendees upon entering, and [then] singles out his teacher with his greeting. Likewise, he bids farewell to him and [the assembly in general] when he departs.

The student does not step over others and sits wherever the assembly's perimeter happens to be, unless the shaykh gives him permission to come forward, or he knows from his shaykh's behavior that he prefers it. He does not let someone rise from his place [out of deference].

He does not sit between two companions except with their permission, and if they make room for him, he sits and squeezes himself in.

We relate that the commander of the faithful, 'Ali ibn Abi Talib (may Allah be pleased with him), said: "The rights the teacher has over you include that you greet others in general but single him out with greetings to the exclusion of the rest. [They also include] sitting in front of him; not pointing with your hand in his company; not winking your eye at someone; not citing an opinion contrary to his; and not backbiting anyone while in his presence. [And they include] not conferring with someone sitting near you while in his audience; not grabbing his garment; not being insistent when he is apprehensive [about something]; and not being disharmonious, such that you become fed up with his company after a length of time."

***Sitting during the Lesson***

The student should also have proper etiquette with his companions and those attending the shaykh's assembly, since this is an extension of having good etiquette with the shaykh and preserves [the dignity of] his assembly. He sits in the presence of the shaykh in the [humble] manner of a student, not that of a teacher. He does not raise his voice exaggeratedly, laugh, or speak much without need. He does not fidget with his hands or the like. He does not turn right or left without need; rather, he faces the shaykh, attentive to his words.

He should not recite to the shaykh while the shaykh is preoccupied or bored, or while he is reluctant, distressed, overjoyed, hungry, thirsty, tired, troubled, or experiencing anything that makes it difficult for him or prevents him from having complete presence of heart or from being energetic. The student should take full advantage of the times when the teacher is energetic.

The student's etiquette includes bearing with the shaykh's coarseness and bad aspects of his character, and not being dissuaded from remaining with him and believing in his expertise. The student offers valid excuses for his shaykh's actions and utterances that outwardly seem flawed. If the shaykh is discourteous towards him, the student takes the initiative to apologize to the shaykh, outwardly showing that the offense is his and that he deserves the reprimand.

***Between Lessons***

The student's etiquette includes [his] determination to study, incessantly doing so any time the opportunity arises. He is not satisfied with little when much is possible. Yet, he does not burden himself with more than he can bear, out of fear of boredom and losing what he has gained. This varies according to each student's character and circumstances.

If the student reaches the place where the shaykh usually sits and does not find him there, he waits patiently for him and stays close to his door. The student does not skip his daily lesson unless out of concern that the shaykh has an aversion [to a given lesson for some reason], since he knows [the shaykh's] preference for being read to at one time and not another. If he finds the shaykh sleeping or occupied with something important, he waits and does not interrupt the shaykh by seeking permission to enter.

The student should take it upon himself to strive hard to achieve [all he can] while he is free of responsibility and energetic—since his body is still strong, and his mind is alert and occupied by few things—before he is confronted with the obstacles of heroism and notoriety.

The student should recite with the shaykh early, at the beginning of the day, because of the hadith of the Prophet (may Allah bless him and grant him peace): "O Allah, bless my nation in its earliness."

We already mentioned that he should not give someone else his turn.

If the shaykh sees benefit in giving others priority at certain times because of a legal reason and he alludes to it, his order should be followed.

***Treating Envy and Pride***

A student is obliged—and strongly advised—to not harbor envy toward his peers or anyone else, because of some good quality that Allah the Generous has given them. Likewise, the student should not boast about anything that he himself achieves.

The way to remove pride is by the student reminding himself that his achievement did not occur through his own power and strength. Rather, it was only through Allah's grace. Therefore, the student should not be proud of something he did not produce—something that Allah Most High placed in him.

The way to overcome envy is to know with certainty that it was the wisdom of Allah Most High that brought a good trait to a person. So one should never object to it; nor should one dislike wisdom that Allah Most High willed and, thus, He Himself does not dislike.

The way to eliminate boasting is to know that it destroys whatever one has in the afterlife and one's blessings in this life, which makes oneself blameworthy.

And to know that, in reality, one does not truly possess anything worthy of aggrandizement.

May Allah spare us His displeasure and grant us success in pleasing Him.

# 5

# *The Etiquette of Bearers of the Quran*

Much of this etiquette has been mentioned in the previous chapter. It includes being in the most complete of states and manifesting the most honorable of qualities through avoidance of everything the Quran prohibits. [It also includes] being protected from ignoble means of income; having dignity; rising above the tyrants and vulgar people of this world; being humble with the righteous, the altruists, and the poor; being fearful [of Allah]; and having tranquility and respect.

'Abdallah ibn Mas'ud (may Allah be pleased with him) said, "The bearer of the Quran should be known by his night when the people are sleeping; by his day when the people are awake; by his sadness when people are joyous; by his weeping when people are laughing; by his silence when people are engrossed [in conversation]; and by his fear when people are pompous."

Al-Hasan al-Basri (may Allah grant him His mercy) said, "The people who came before you considered the Quran to be correspondence from their Lord, so they would ponder it by night and act upon it by day."

Al-Fudayl ibn 'Iyad (may Allah grant him His mercy) said, "The bearer of the Quran is the bearer of the banner of Islam. He should not allow himself to be distracted by someone who distracts himself, nor talk about nonsense with those who talk nonsense—all out of due veneration of the Quran."

### *Reciting as a Means of Livelihood*

It is important to take every precaution not to use the Quran for one's livelihood and earn income with it. Statements regarding its prohibition are numerous and well known, including hadiths from the Prophet (may Allah bless him and grant him peace), and statements from the Companions (may Allah be pleased with them) and the Righteous Forebearers (may Allah be pleased with them and grant them His mercy).

The scholars disagree about the issue of taking wages for teaching the Quran. Imams 'Ata', Malik, al-Shafi'i, and others permitted taking wages provided that there was a valid agreement. Al-Zuhri, Abu Hanifa, and others prohibited it. (May Allah grant them all His mercy.)

Rigorously authenticated hadiths have been related indicating its permissibility. I clarified two responses to the hadiths indicating its prohibition [in *Al-Tibyan*], along with other answers to the issue.[2]

### *Continually Completing the Quran*

A person should maintain consistency in his recitation and perform it often. The Righteous Forebearers (may Allah be pleased with them and grant them His mercy)

2. Al-Nawawi, *Etiquette with the Quran,* (n.a., Islamosaic: 2012), p28.

had different habits regarding when they would finish [the Quran]. Some would complete it once every two months or every month; others, once every ten nights or every eight; some, every seven nights; others, every six nights or every five; some, every day and night, twice every day and night, twice each day, thrice each day, and four times each day. Most would complete the Quran every seven nights, and many, every three. I clarified each of these groups in *Al-Tibyan,* along with their evidences.[3]

The preferred opinion is that [the amount one reads] may vary from person to person. If someone finds subtleties and experiences [insight] by way of profound reflection, then he should limit [himself] to the amount [of reading] that would enable him to obtain full understanding of what he reads. This applies to anyone occupied with transmitting knowledge or anything else important to the religion and to the general welfare of Muslims: one limits [oneself] to that which does not overburden one's capacity. Yet, if one is not among these [transmitters], then one should do as much as possible but not to the point of tedium and abandoning one's recitation.

It is best to complete [the recitation] at the beginning of the day or night. It is also said that it is best to complete the recitation once by night and another time by day. When completing it by day, it should be during the two prayer-cycles of the Morning Prayer, or afterwards. And when completing it by night, it should

3. Ibid., pp28–31.

be during the two recommend prayer-cycles associated with the Sunset Prayer, or afterwards.

[The Prophet (may Allah bless him and grant him peace) said,] "Whoever completes the Quran during the day, the angels will pray for him until dawn. If his completion coincides with the end of the night, the angels pray for him until [the following] night."

### *Reciting at Night*

One should take care to recite the Quran mostly at night, and primarily during prayer at night. Praying and reciting at night [in solitude] are preponderant because [at that time], one is most primed for the composure of one's heart and removed from preoccupations, entertainment, and attending to needs. Also, one is safe-guarded from ostentation and other acts that reduce reward. This is in addition to what the Sacred Law has conveyed about the tremendous benefit that can be found at night. Indeed, the Messenger's Miraculous Journey occurred at night (may Allah bless him and grant him peace), and there are hadiths [extolling its virtues]: "Every night, your Lord descends to the lowest heaven," and "At night, there is an hour in which Allah answers every supplication. It [occurs] every night."

The Quran, Prophetic traditions, and the consensus of our scholars, all clearly indicate the superiority of reciting and praying at night. The blessings from praying at night and reciting [the Quran] are attained with little or much [recitation]. However, the more one increases [one's acts of devotion], the better [it is], unless they completely fill the night, since it is offensive to always do so and such a habit may cause harm to oneself.

The Messenger of Allah (may Allah bless him and grant him peace) said, "Whoever stood [at night] for ten *ayahs* [verses] will not be written among the heedless. Whoever stood for one hundred *ayahs* is written among the obedient. Whoever stood for one thousand *ayahs* is written among those with immense wealth." (Abu Dawud)

If one slept through all or part of his nightly litany of recitation [*hizb*], he should read it at the beginning of the day. Umar ibn al-Khattab (may Allah be pleased with him) related that the Messenger of Allah (may Allah bless him and grant him peace) said, "Whoever slept through all or part of his nightly litany of recitation but read it between the Morning and Afternoon Prayers, it is written for him as if he had read it at night." (Muslim)

### *The Importance of Retaining the Quran*

One must take every precaution to avoid forgetting the Quran or even part of it, and not put oneself at risk of forgetting it.

The Messenger of Allah (may Allah bless him and grant him peace) said, "The rewards of my nation were shown to me—even the litter a man removes from the mosque. And the sins of my nation were shown to me. I did not see a sin greater than a chapter [*surah*] or verse [*ayah*] of the Quran given to a person who then forgot it." (Abu Dawud and others)

The Prophet (may Allah bless him and grant him peace) said, "Whoever reads the Quran and then forgets it meets Allah Mighty and Majestic on the Day of Judgment [while he is] disfigured."

# 6

# *The Etiquette of Recitation*

The first things that are obligatory for the reciter are sincerity, as previously stated, and observing proper etiquette with the Quran. One should be aware that one is addressing Allah Mighty and Majestic, and should therefore read as if one sees Allah Most High.

***The Toothstick***

If one wants to recite the Quran, one should clean one's mouth with a toothstick [*miswak*] or the like. The preference is for the toothstick to be a twig from the arak tree. It is permissible to use other twigs or anything that cleans, such as a coarse cloth or saltwort.

[Proper cleaning] cannot be accomplished with a coarse finger, according to the soundest opinion. According to another opinion, it [is acceptable] if nothing else is available.

One brushes laterally with the toothstick, beginning from the right side, with the intention of performing a sunnah.

One passes the toothstick along the outer and inner portions of the teeth, and gently passes the toothstick over the roof of one's palate. One should use an ordinary toothstick, not [one] that is extremely dry or wet. There is no problem with using someone else's toothstick, with his permission.

When one's mouth is filthy with blood or the like, one should rinse it. It is offensive to recite the Quran without doing so; and Imam al-Shafi'i's colleagues (may Allah grant them His mercy) transmit two opinions concerning it being unlawful.

***Ritual Purity***

It is recommended to be in a state of ritual purity when reciting the Quran. It is permissible to recite in a state of minor ritual impurity, according to the consensus of the Muslims. One should not say that one has committed an offensive act [if one recites with minor ritual impurity]. Rather, one has neglected what is best. If one does not find water, one should make dry ablution [*tayammum*]. The ruling concerning a woman with abnormal vaginal bleeding who is otherwise considered pure, is similar to that of anyone with minor ritual impurity.

It is unlawful for a person in a state of major ritual impurity or during menstruation to recite the Quran, whether it is a verse or even less. It is permissible for them to silently peruse the Quran in their hearts without uttering it, and to look in the actual text of the Quran [*mushaf*] and to go over it in their hearts.

The Muslims have consensus that it is permissible for a person in a state of major ritual impurity and during menstruation to say, "*Subhan Allah,*" "*La ilaha illa Allah,*" "*Al-Hamdu li-Llah,*" "*Allahu akbar,*" to offer prayers and salutations upon the Messenger of Allah (may Allah bless him and grant him peace), and recite other litanies.

Our Shafi'i companions (may Allah grant them His mercy) said that it is permissible [while in a state of impurity] for one person to say to another, "O Yahya! Hold fast to the Book," (Quran, 19:12), or the like. It is also permissible, when mounting a riding beast, to say, "Glory be to Him who has subjugated this for us, otherwise we could not have subdued them," (Quran, 43:13), and when supplicating, "Lord! Give us what is good in this world and what is good in the Hereafter; and keep us from the torment of the Fire," (Quran, 2:201).

And it is permissible to say, "In the name of Allah," and "Praise be to Allah."

[It is permissible to utter the aforementioned supplications when one is in a state of major ritual impurity or menstruating] if one does not intend them as recitation of the Quran. But if one intends recitation with any of them, one has sinned.[4]

### *Dry Ablution*

An individual with major ritual impurity or who is menstruating may make dry ablution [*tayammum*] in the absence of water. Then it would be lawful to recite Quran, pray, and perform other acts [that require ritual purity]. But if thereafter, one were to have minor

---

4. I have omitted an issue here related to abrogation that is not of practical value to English readers. Interested readers may refer to *Etiquette with the Quran,* p37 and its corresponding footnote on p138.

ritual impurity, it would be unlawful to pray, but not unlawful to recite [Quran].

Regarding this issue, there is no difference between making dry ablution while a resident or while traveling. Some have mentioned that if one makes dry ablution while a resident, it is lawful to pray, but one may not recite [Quran] outside the prayer nor sit in the mosque. But the sound position is that [reciting] is permissible, as we previously mentioned.

When someone with major ritual impurity finds neither earth nor water [with which to attain purification], he may [still] perform prayer, but it would be unlawful for him to recite [Quran] beyond prayer bounds. During the prayer itself, it would be unlawful to recite any Quran other than Al-Fatihah. Another opinion deems it unlawful to recite Al-Fatihah [in this situation] and instead, one should recite the litanies that an incapacitated person who has not memorized anything from the Quran would recite. The first opinion is correct.

### *Place of Recitation*

It is recommended that recitation [of the Quran] occur in a carefully chosen and clean place. Because of this, a group of scholars recommended reciting in the mosque, since it combines cleanliness and nobility; and it achieves the benefit of spiritual retreat [*i'tikaf*]. Anyone who sits in a mosque should intend spiritual retreat, whether he sits for a short or long duration. He should intend such a spiritual retreat upon entering the mosque.

Concerning reciting in a bathhouse, our Shafi'i companions said that it is not offensive. 'Ata, Ibrahim al-Nakha'i and Malik held the same opinion. However, Abu Hanifa and other scholars declared it offensive. (May Allah grant them all His mercy.)

Al-Sha'bi (may Allah grant him His mercy) said that it is offensive to read the Quran in three locations: bathhouses, lavatories, and in mill-houses while the stone is turning.

As for reciting while travelling, the preferred opinion is that it is permissible and not offensive, as long as the reciter is not distracted. A similar opinion was conveyed from Darda' (may Allah be pleased with him) and 'Umar ibn 'Abd al-'Aziz (may Allah grant him His mercy). And it was conveyed that Imam Malik disliked it (may Allah grant him His mercy).

### *Facing the Direction of Prayer*

It is recommended for the reciter who is not praying to face the direction of prayer. He sits with humility, tranquility, and dignity, while lowering his head. He sits alone, to perfect his etiquette and humility—as he does when sitting before his teacher. This is the most complete way to recite. If he were to read while standing, reclining on his side, in bed, or in some other bearing, it would be permissible, and he would receive a reward, though of a lesser degree than the former [postures]. The evidence for all of this is mentioned in the Quran and well-known Prophetic traditions.

### *Seeking Protection*

When one intends to begin one's recitation, one first seeks protection by saying, "*A'udhu billahi min al-shaytan al-rajim*" ["I seek protection by Allah from the accursed Devil"]. If instead, one were to say, "I seek refuge in Allah, the All-Hearing, the All-Knowing, from the accursed Devil," there would be nothing wrong with it. But the first way is preferred, and it is what the vast majority says.

Seeking protection is recommended but not obligatory. It is recommended for every reciter, whether in prayer or not. It is recommended at [the beginning of] each prayer-cycle, according to the soundest opinion. According to the another opinion, it is only recommended in the first prayer-cycle, so if one neglected it then, one says it in the second.

It is recommended to seek refuge after the inaugural "*Allahu akbar*" is said in the Funeral Prayer, according to the soundest opinion.

One seeks refuge audibly when reciting outside of prayer. There are two possibilities regarding whether it should be said aloud in prayers that have audible recitation.

### *Saying "Bismillahi al-Rahman al-Rahim"*

One should take care to recite [the *basmala,*] which is "*Bismillahi al-Rahman al-Rahim*" ["In the name of Allah, Most Merciful and Compassionate,"] at the beginning of each *surah* [of the Quran,] except for Surat al-Bara' [i.e., Surat al-Tawba] (9). Most scholars consider [the *basmala*] to be a verse [of the Quran] since it is written in the text of the Quran and has always been written in the beginning of all *surah*s except al-Bara'. So if one recites it, one achieves a complete recitation [of the whole Quran] or, of a whole *surah*. But if one omits it, then—according to the majority of scholars—one has neglected part of the Quran. If the recitation is part of a service that involves wages—such as reciting a seventh of the Quran [*subu'*] or a thirtieth [*juz'*] in exchange for compensation from an endowment—extra care must be taken to ensure that the *basmala* is read, so that the reciter will be deserving of the wage he receives, for if he were to omit it, he would not deserve anything from the endowment, according to those who say that the phrase "*Bismillahi al-Rahman al-Rahim*" is a verse at the beginning of each *surah* (and they are the majority). People are lax when it comes to this fine point, so it merits additional attention and prominence.

### ***Humility and Pondering***

At the beginning of and during the recitation, one's state should be that of humility and reflection. [This state] is the desired objective, through which breasts are opened and hearts illuminated.

Allah Mighty and Majestic said, "[This is] a Book that We have sent down to you, full of blessing, that they may reflect upon its signs," (Quran, 38:29); and "Will they not reflect upon the Quran?" (Quran, 4:82). The hadiths and non-Prophetic reports concerning this topic are numerous.

A number of Righteous Forebearers (may Allah be

pleased with them and grant them His mercy) spent one night reciting a single verse, pondering and repeating it until the morning. A number of them were overwhelmed while reciting [it], and some actually died. I mentioned several reports in *Al-Tibyan* concerning these individuals (may Allah grant them His mercy).[5]

Ibrahim al-Khawwas (may Allah be pleased with him), the noble master of spiritual gifts and experiences, said: "There are five medicines for the heart: reciting the Quran with reflection, emptying the stomach, standing at night [in prayer], supplicating during the last part of the night, and sitting with the righteous."

***Weeping during Recitation***

Know that weeping during recitation is recommended. It is a trait of those who possess profound knowledge of Allah, and is a distinguishing feature of Allah's righteous devotees. Allah Most High said, "They fall down upon their faces weeping, and it increases them in humility," (Quran, 17:109).

Many hadiths and accounts from the Righteous Forebearers (may Allah be pleased with them and grant them His mercy) have been related concerning this. I pointed to some of them in *Al-Tibyan*.[6]

The way to achieve this state is by bringing sadness to mind by pondering the threats and warnings, and the covenants and agreements contained in the Quran, and then contemplating one's shortcomings with regard

---

5. Ibid., pp42–43.
6. Ibid., pp44–45.

to them. If this does not elicit sadness and provoke weeping, then one should weep from its absence, since it is among the greatest of calamities.

### *Reciting Distinctly*

One should recite distinctly. The scholars (may Allah be well pleased with them) are in agreement that distinct recitation is recommended. Allah Most High said, "And recite the Quran distinctly," (Quran, 73:4).

It is established in rigorously-authenticated hadiths that the recitation of the Messenger of Allah (may Allah bless him and grant him peace) was distinct, letter by letter. And so were the recitations of the Righteous Forebearers (may Allah be pleased with them and grant them His mercy).

Reciting rapidly with excessive haste, called "*hadhrama*" [in Arabic], is prohibited.

The scholars say that reciting a given amount of the Quran slowly is superior to reciting double its amount in the same allotted time.

They also say that reciting slowly is recommended for the sake of understanding, and because it is closer to veneration and respect, and has a far greater impact on the heart. And it is for these [latter] reasons that a slow, distinct recitation is recommended for a foreigner who does not understand the Quran's meanings.

### *Supplicating While Reciting*

Whenever one encounters a verse containing the mention of mercy, it is recommended to ask Allah Most

High from His bounty. Whenever one comes across a verse containing the mention of chastisement, one seeks protection with Allah from evil or from chastisement or says, "*Allahumma inni as'aluka al-'afiyyah*" ["O Allah, I ask You for well-being"], "[*Allahumma inni*] *as'aluka al-mu'afa min kulli makruh*" ["I ask You for exemption from every disliked thing"], or similar [supplications].

When one arrives at a verse declaring Allah Most High transcendent beyond any imperfection, one should declare Him transcendent beyond imperfection by saying, "*Subhanahu wa ta'ala*" ["He is Transcendent and Most High"], "*Tabarak wa ta'ala*" ["He is Blessed and Most High"], or "*Jallat 'azamatu rabbina*" ["Glorified is our Lord's greatness"].

This is recommended for the one leading a congregation [in prayer], following an imam, or praying individually. And this is established as the practice of the Messenger of Allah (may Allah grant him and give him peace) [in rigorously-authenticated reports]. (Muslim)

***Reciting in a Foreign Language***

It is not permissible to recite the Quran in any language [other than Arabic], regardless of the reciter's level of proficiency in Arabic or whether the recitation takes place during prayer or at other times. If one recites the Quran in a foreign language during prayer, one's prayer is invalid. This is the school of Malik, al-Shafi'i, Ahmad, and Dawud. Abu Hanifa said that it is permissible; and his two companions [Abu Yusuf and Muhammad al-Shaybani] said it is [only] permissible for someone who is not versed in Arabic. (May Allah grant them all His mercy.)

***Permissible Recitations***

It is permissible to recite [the Quran] using any of the seven universally accepted recitations. It is not permissible to use any other, such as the *shadh* [anomalous] accounts transmitted from the seven reciters. If one were to recite with the *shadh* in his prayer, one's prayer would be invalid, provided one was aware [of the ruling forbidding it]. If one was ignorant of it, then the prayer is valid, but one is not rewarded for the recitation.

***Switching Recitations***

If one begins to recite using one accepted recitation, one should not interrupt it while the [recited] words remain connected. One may, however, switch to reciting with another of the seven recitations once the words are no longer connected [i.e., at a natural pause]. But it is better to continue with the first recitation throughout the sitting.

***Reciting in Order***

The scholars say that it is better to recite according to the order of the Quranic text [*mushaf*]. (For example, one recites Al-Fatihah [1], then Al-Baqarah [2], then Al-'Imran [3], then Al-Nisa' [4] and so forth, until ending with Al-Nas [114].) This applies whether one recites during prayer or outside of it.

Likewise, if one recites a *surah*, it is recommended to recite the one that follows it. So if one recited Al-Nas (114) in the first prayer-cycle, one should recite Al-Baqarah (2) in the second prayer-cycle.

This ruling is supported by the fact that the order of the Quranic text was arranged in this manner, purely out of divine wisdom. So one should strive to preserve [the order], diverging from it only when the Sacred Law mentions exceptions, such as the Morning Prayer on Friday, during which one recites Surat al-Sajdah (32) in the first prayer-cycle and Surat al-Insan (76) in the second; and the Eid Prayer, during which Surat Qaf (50) is recited in the first prayer-cycle and Surat al-Qamr (54) in the second. Other examples will come in the eighth chapter, if Allah Most High so wills.

It is permissible to forgo the order by reading a *surah* that does not immediately follow another or by reading a *surah* and then another before it, though this neglects what is best.

As for reciting a *surah* from its end to its beginning, there is agreement that it is forbidden and blameworthy, since it removes aspects of [the Quran's] inimitability and negates the wisdom invested in the specific ordering of the *ayah*s.

Teaching children from the end of the text [moving] toward its beginning is fine and not relevant to this discussion since it is a discontinuous recitation spread over several days.

***Reciting from the Mushaf or from Memory***

Reciting the Quran from the *mushaf* is better than reciting it from memory, since it combines reciting with looking. And according to our Shafi'i colleagues and the Righteous Forebearers (may Allah be pleased with them and grant them His mercy), looking at the written text of the Quran is a kind of worship, and I myself do not see any disagreement therein. But perhaps they mean that reciting from the *mushaf* is preferable for one who finds veneration [of Allah] and contemplation [of the Quran] equally attainable whether reading from the text or reciting from memory, while reciting from memory is preferable for someone whose veneration and contemplation are greater when doing so.

***Devotion to the Quran in a Group***

Know that group recitation is a recommended act, as is attending their circles. The rewards for the one who gathers them to recite are immense, and he is among those striving towards proper etiquette with the Quran and maintaining its rights. All of these are established with evidences.

The Prophet (may Allah bless him and grant him peace) said, "A group does not gather in one of the houses of Allah Most High reciting the Quran and studying it together, except that tranquility descends upon them, mercy envelops them, the angels encompass them, and Allah mentions them to those in His presence." [Muslim; Abu Dawud]

In *Al-Tibyan*, I mentioned reports from the Prophet (may Allah bless him and grant him peace) and others regarding this.[7]

There are two good ways to read together. The first way is for the whole group to read everything together, in unison. The second way is for some of them to recite a thirtieth, for example, while the others remain silent. Then, the ones who were silent recite while the ones who had recited listen on. This [latter method] is known as "reciting in rounds."

### *Proper Etiquette for Group Recitations*

The etiquettes that must be followed when reciting in a group are numerous and it is not possible to mention them exhaustively in this section. However, we will mention some that will point to the rest.

Everything that an individual observes when reciting alone must be observed when reciting in a group. And we add to those several etiquettes that some ignorant reciters may neglect. [The emphasized etiquette] includes avoiding laughing, clamor, and conversing during a recitation, fidgeting with the hands or the like, and looking at what distracts and scatters the mind. More abhorrent than all of these is looking at what is generally impermissible, like looking at a minor who is on the verge of adulthood. Looking at a minor on the verge of adulthood who is attractive is unlawful, even if one looks without lust, and even if one feels secure from temptation. This is the sound, preferred opinion according to the accomplished scholars. [...] Allah Most High says, "Tell the believing men to lower their gaze and guard their private parts," (Quran,

7. Ibid., pp52–53.

24:30). Such an individual [i.e., an attractive minor] is similar to an adult—and many are even more attractive [...], —so looking at them is even more inappropriate and unlawful. The Righteous Forebearers (may Allah be pleased with them and grant them His mercy) have made innumerable statements advising their avoidance.[8]

If someone attending an assembly for recitation sees one of the forbidden things we've mentioned or something like it, he must forbid it to whatever extent possible: either with his hand, if he is able, with his tongue if unable with his hand but able with words, and if unable [with the hand or tongue], he censures it with his heart.

### *Reciting with a Raised Voice*

This section is important and should be given particular attention. Know that there are many hadiths found in *Sahih al-Bukhari, Sahih Muslim,* and other hadith compendiums indicating that it is recommended to raise one's voice when reciting, while others state that it is recommended to hush the recitation and lower the voice. Some of the Righteous Forebearers (may Allah be pleased with them and grant them His mercy) preferred lowering the voice, while other preferred raising it.

---

8. In the original, Imam al-Nawawi mentions a particular instance of a general problem. I have adjusted the text to fit with the general problem since it is of greater practical value to today's reader.

The scholars say that the way to reconcile these [seemingly] conflicting narrations and accounts is [to know] that making [one's recitation] secret further removes one from ostentation and is thus better for someone who fears it. If one does not fear ostentation in reciting audibly and raising the voice, then being audible and raising the voice is better, since there is more effort involved and its benefit extends to others [who may hear it]. And benefit that extends to others is better than personal benefit [alone]. Also, [audible recitation] awakens the heart of the reciter, gathers his attentiveness, directs him to reflect upon [what he reads], draws his hearing to it, repels sleep, and invigorates [the mind]. It also rouses and energizes those who are asleep or inattentive. Scholars have said that whenever one brings to mind all of these intentions, audible recitation is better. And if these intentions are combined, the reward is duly increased. This is when one does not fear ostentatious show or other vices, and when one will not annoy or confuse others who are engaged in prayer.

If the recitation is from a group gathered together, it is emphatically recommended that every reciter raise his voice.

I mentioned reports from the Prophet (may Allah bless him and grant him peace) and others related to this section in *Al-Tibyan*.[9]

9. Ibid., pp53–57.

**_Beautifying One's Voice with Quran_**

The scholars of the earlier generations, including the Companions, the Successors, and later Muslim scholars and leaders from various regions (may Allah be pleased with them and grant them His Mercy) are in agreement that it is recommended to beautify one's voice when reciting the Quran. The statements and actions [in support of this] are well known, and the hadiths of the Messenger of Allah (may Allah bless him and grant him peace) are widely circulated among the general public and the elite.

The scholars (may Allah grant then His mercy have said that it is recommended to beautify the voice and adorn it during recitation, as long as it does not exceed the proper limits of recitation by being overly prolonged. If [the recitation] is exaggerated such that a letter is added or is muffled, then it is unlawful. It is [also] unlawful for a listener to remain silent when he is capable of objecting to it. [It is unlawful] because it deviates the Quran's straight manner to what is crooked. Allah Most High says, "It is a Quran in Arabic, without any crookedness," (Quran, 39:28).

Another example of reciting using unlawful melodies is the manner in which some ignoble fools recite the Quran at funerals and various festivals. This is a manifestly unlawful innovation and may Allah the Noble hasten its elimination.

Al-Shafi'i (may Allah grant him His mercy) says, "The best recitation is one that is slow and sorrowful." A recitation is "slow" when it is prolonged. And it is said that one recites with sorrow by softening one's voice.

Abu Hurayrah (may Allah be pleased with him) recited in a manner that was sorrowful, resembling a dirge.

If one's voice is not beautiful, one should beautify it as much as one is able.

### *Seeking a Wholesome, Beautiful Recitation*

Know that many among the Righteous Forebearers (may Allah be pleased with them and grant them His mercy) would ask those with beautiful voices to recite while they listened on. There is agreement that this is recommended. It is the habit of the elite, devoted, and righteous worshippers of Allah, and it is an established sunnah of the Prophet (may Allah bless him and grant him peace).

The Messenger of Allah (may Allah bless him and grant him peace) told Ibn Mas'ud (may Allah be pleased with him): "Recite the Quran to me." Ibn Mas'ud read Surat al-Nisa' until the verse, "How will it be when We bring a witness from every nation, and We bring you [O Muhammad] as a witness against these [people]," (Quran, 4:41). The Prophet (may Allah bless him and grant him peace) said, "Enough." Ibn Mas'ud (may Allah be pleased with him) then turned to the Prophet (may Allah bless him and grant him peace) and saw his eyes brimming with tears. (Bukhari; Muslim)

The accounts concerning this are well known and numerous. Some among the Righteous Forebearers have actually died as a result of the [powerful] recitations of those whom they had asked to recite. (May

Allah be pleased with them and grant them His mercy.)

The scholars recommend that an assembly gathered [to hear or study] the hadiths of the Prophet (may Allah bless him and grant him peace) should commence and conclude with a recitation of a brief passage from the Quran by a reciter with a beautiful voice. In these contexts, one should recite what is appropriate and suitable for the assembly. One's recitation should include *ayahs* in which there is hope, fear, and exhortation; [the merits of] abstinence from this world and desire for the hereafter; the diminishing of vain hopes; and [the importance of] having noble character.

### *Reading What Has Complete Meaning*

When the reciter begins in the middle of a *surah* or does not stop at its end, he should start from the previous words [of the *surah*] that are related to one another [in meaning]. The same applies when the reciter stops on words that are related or that come at the end of a dialogue. When beginning and stopping, the reciter should not limit himself to [strict textual divisions of the Quran, like stopping or starting at] tenths, sixtieths, and thirtieths [of the text], since he might be in the middle of an interrelated passage, like the following thirtieths [of the Quran], which contain words of the Most High [that impart meaning only when read with what is connected to them]: "And all the married women...," (Quran, 4:24); [Joseph said,] "I do not claim innocence for my soul...," (Quran, 12:53); and "What is your errand, O Messengers?" (Quran, 51:31).

The reciter should not begin or stop at any of these [places] or their like, since they are related in meaning to what came before them. People should not be deceived by reciters who ignore this etiquette and do not ponder these meanings!

Because of this, the scholars have said that reciting a short *surah* in its entirety is better than reciting the same amount of a larger *surah*, since the interrelatedness [of its meanings] may be hidden to some people in some circumstances. The Righteous Forebearers (may Allah be pleased with them and grant them His mercy) disliked it when reciters would read only part of a verse and omit the rest of it. And Allah knows best.

### *When It Is Offensive to Read the Quran*

Know that reciting the Quran, in general, is unconditionally recommended, except during specific circumstances wherein the Sacred Law has prohibited its recitation. I will now mention the circumstances that come to my mind.

It is offensive to recite while one is bowing, prostrating, [saying the] *tashahhud,* and at other stations of the prayer other than standing.

It is offensive [to recite] while relieving oneself, while drowsy, or during any similar circumstance in which the Quran becomes unintelligible to oneself [or others].

It is offensive to recite [while the imam is delivering] the Friday sermon if one is able to hear it. However, it is not offensive for someone who is unable to hear [the sermon]. Rather, it is recommended. This is the sound and preferred opinion.

It is offensive for someone following an imam to recite anything in addition to Al-Fatihah during an audible prayer, [that is, the Dawn, Sunset, and Nightfall Prayers], if he is able to hear the imam's recitation. But it is recommended for him to recite aloud if he cannot hear the imam.

It is not offensive to recite while circling the Ka'ba.

The discussion on the difference concerning reciting in a bathhouse and along a road [that one travels], and concerning one whose mouth is unclean, has already been addressed.

***Rejected Innovations***

One of the rejected innovations regarding the recitation [of the Quran] is what the ignorant do when praying Tarawih Prayers among common folk: they recite Surat al-An'am (6) in the final prayer-cycle of the seventh night,[10] believing that it is recommended. They combine several rejected matters, which I clarified in *Al-Tibyan*.[11]

Some ignorant people engage in a similar innovation during the Morning Prayer on Friday, deliberately reciting [a passage of the Quran that calls for] prostration other than Surat al-Sajdah (32), while the Sunnah is to recite Surat al-Sajdah in the first prayer-cycle, and Surat al-Insan (76) in the second.

---

10. The text mentions "fourth." I have replaced it with "seventh" as is mentioned in multiple copies of *Al-Tibyan*.
11. Ibid., p62.

### *Miscellaneous Issues of Concern*

If one happens to pass wind while one is reciting [outside of prayer], then one should cease reciting until it completely exits, and then one may resume.

If one yawns, one should cease reciting until one finishes yawning and then resume.

It is good etiquette that one lower one's voice when reciting certain statements of Allah Mighty and Majestic, as in the following *ayahs*: "The Jews say, 'Ezṛa is the son of Allah,' and the Christians say, 'The Messiah is the son of Allah,'" (Quran, 9:30); "The Jews say, 'Allah's hand is fettered,'" (Quran, 5:64); "They say, 'The All-Merciful has begotten a son,'" (Quran, 19:88). This is what Ibrahim al-Nakha'i (may Allah grant him His mercy) would do.

If someone recites, "Allah and His angels bless the Prophet. O you who believe, bless him and salute him with a worthy salutation," (Quran, 33:56), one should pray that Allah bless the Prophet and grant him peace.

If someone recites, "Is not Allah the best of judges?" (Quran, 95:8) or "Is He then not able to raise the dead to life?" (Quran, 75:40), one should say, "*Bala wa ana 'ala dhalika min al-shahidin*" ["Most certainly! And I am among those who bear witness to this!"].

And if someone recites, "In what words after this will they believe?" (Quran, 7:185), one should say, "*Amantu bi-llah*" ["I believe in Allah!"].

And if someone recites Surat al-A'la (87) [one should say, "*Subhana rabbi al-A'la*" ("Transcendent is my Lord, Most Exalted, above all imperfections!")].

And if someone recites, "Praise to Allah, who has not taken a son," (Quran, 17:111) [one should say, "*al-hamdu lillah alladhi lam yattakhidh walada*" ("Praise be to Allah who has not begotten a son!")].

***Reciting the Quran Intending It to Be Speech***

There is disagreement concerning whether it is offensive to recite the Quran with the intention of it being speech.

If a person seeks permission [to enter] from someone who is in prayer, and the person praying then recites, "Enter it with safety and security," (Quran, 15:46)—whether he intended thereby only recitation or both recitation and notification [to the person seeking permission]—it does not nullify his prayer. But if he intended notification alone and the intention [for recitation] did not occur to him, his prayer is nullified. This is what our Shafi'i colleagues have said (may Allah grant them His mercy).

***A Reciter Giving Greetings***

If one recites while walking and then comes across other people, it is recommended to interrupt the recitation, greet them, and then resume one's recitation. And if [upon resuming,] one repeats the [supplication] seeking protection from Allah, it is excellent. If one were sitting [as one recites] and someone passes by, one should do the same—according to the most apparent opinion.

It is obligatory for a reciter to reply [to someone's greetings] with an utterance [of some kind].

Our colleague Imam al-Wahidi (may Allah grant him His mercy) said that it is best to refrain from greeting someone who is reciting; and if someone greets [the reciter], it is sufficient for him to reply with a gesture.

If one sneezes while reciting, it is recommended that one say, "*Al-Hamdu lillah*" ["Praise to Allah"]; and to say to someone else [who has sneezed], "*Yarhamakumu llah*" ["May Allah be merciful with you"].

If a reciter hears someone make the Call to Prayer [*adhan*] or the Call for the Commencement of Prayer [*iqamah*], he should interrupt his recitation and reply to the call [as established in the Sunnah] by repeating its phrases.

If something is requested from a person reciting the Quran and it is possible for him to respond to the petitioner by way of a known gesture, and [the reciter] knows that it will not break the [petitioner's] heart, nor harm their friendship and the like, then it is better to answer by way of a gesture and not interrupt the recitation. But it is permissible for [the reciter] to interrupt [his recitation].

If someone of superior knowledge, righteousness, nobility, old age, or prestige through social status, parentage, or some other factor, passes by someone who is reciting, there is no harm in the reciter standing [to greet him] out of respect and deference.

### *Several Surahs in One Prayer-Cycle*

There is no harm in joining *surahs* in a single prayer-cycle.

It is recommended for the imam leading an audible prayer to remain silent during four periods while standing: First, silence after the opening "*Allahu akbar*," in order to make an opening supplication and so the followers may also say the opening "*Allahu akbar*"; second, a very brief pause right before reciting Surat al-Fatihah and [a brief pause] between the completion of Al-Fatihah and saying "*Amin*" so that "*Amin*" is not misconstrued and thought to be part of Al-Fatihah; third, a long pause after "*Amin*" so the followers themselves can [silently] read Al-Fatihah; and fourth, after finishing [the recitation of] a *surah* of the Quran, in order to provide a separation between the recitation and saying "*Allahu akbar*" before descending to bow.

***Saying "Amin"***

It is recommended for every reciter, whether during prayer or other times, to say "*Amin*" when finishing Al-Fatihah.

Four pronunciations for "Amin" are mentioned: [The first two] involve elongating and shortening [the *alif*] and lightening the *mim* ["*Āmīn*" and "*Amīn*"]. A third opinion is pronouncing "*Amin*" with *imala* [in which the *alif* is pronounced like the *ya*] with elongation between the two; al-Wahidi conveys this from Hamza and al-Kisa'i (may Allah grant them His mercy). The fourth opinion posits that the *mim* has a *shaddah* [i.e., the phoneme is doubled]with an elongated *alif* ["*Āmmīn*"]; al-Wahidi conveys this from al-Hasan al-Basri and al-Husayn ibn al-Fadl (may Allah grant them His mercy). However, the masses [of lexicographers] reject the latter opinion of there being a *shadda*.

The end of the *nun* does not have a vowel. But

when it is connected with what follows, the *nun* gets a *fatha* because of the consecutiveness of two silent letters, just like it is given a *fatha* in [the words] *'ayn* and *kayf* [*'ayna, kayfa*], and not given a *kasra* since *kasra* is heavy after *ya*.

Approximately fifteen meanings have been mentioned for "*Amin*." The best-known and apparent meaning is "O Allah, answer!"

The scholars have said that saying "*Amin*" in prayer is recommended for the imam, his followers, and for individuals [praying alone]. The imam and the individual [praying alone] should audibly pronounce "*Amin*" in the audible prayers.

The follower saying "*Amin*" should say it simultaneously with the imam—not before or after him.

### *Prostration during Recitation of Quranic Ayahs*

This topic is among the emphasized matters that one should give particular attention to. The scholars have consensus concerning the command to prostrate during the recitation of [certain passages of] the Quran, but they disagree whether this command indicates that it is recommended or obligatory. Abu Hanifa (may Allah grant him His mercy) considered the prostration to be obligatory. 'Umar ibn al-Khattab, Ibn 'Abbas, Salman al-Farisi, 'Imran ibn al-Husayn, Malik, al-Awza'i, al-Shafi'i, Ahmad, Ishaq, Abu Thawr, Dawud, and others said that it is recommended and not obligatory per se. (May Allah be pleased with them and grant them His mercy.)

***The Number of Ayahs of Prostration and Their Places***

As for their number, the preferred opinion of al-Shafi'i (may Allah grant him His mercy) and the majority of scholars is that there are fourteen *ayahs* of prostration: Al-A'raf (7:206); Al-Ra'd (13:15); Al-Nahl (16:49-50); Al-Isra' (17:107-09); Maryam (19:58); two in al-Hajj (22:18), (22:77); Al-Furqan (25:60); Al-Naml (27:25-26); Al-Sajdah (32:15); Fussilat (41:37-38); Al-Najm (53:62); Al-Inshiqaq (84:21); and Al-'Alaq (96:19).

These are the emphatically recommended prostrations.

As for the prostration of Surat Sad (38:24), it is recommended but not considered among the emphatically recommended prostrations.

The specific locations of these prostrations are well known. There is no disagreement as to their specific locations [in the *surahs*], except for Fussilat (41). The opinion of Abu Hanifa, al-Shafi'i, Ahmad, and many of the Righteous Forebearers (may Allah be pleased with them and grant them His mercy) is that it occurs immediately after Allah's statement, "...and are never wearied," (Quran, 41:38).

Malik and many of the Righteous Forebearers, including 'Umar ibn al-Khattab (may Allah be pleased with them and grant them His mercy), hold that it occurs immediately after Allah's statement, " ...if you would worship Him," (Quran, 41:37). This is also an opinion of one or more of the companions of Imam al-Shafi'i (may Allah grant them His mercy). But the correct opinion is the first, and it is more precautionary.

As for the location of the prostration in Al-Naml (27), the correct and well-known opinion is that it occurs at the statement of Allah Most High, "Lord of the formidable Throne" (Quran, 27:26). Al-'Abdari, one of our Shafi'i companions (may Allah grant him His mercy), said that it occurs at the saying of Allah Most High, "...and knows what you conceal and what you reveal," (Quran, 27:25), and he claimed that this is the opinion of our school and of most of the legal scholars. This is a manifest error; the correct opinion is what we mentioned earlier.

***About Surat Sad***

If one who recites [verse 24] of Surat Sad (38) outside of prayer, it is recommended for him to prostrate. But if one recites it during prayer, he should not prostrate. If, however, one does prostrate out of ignorance or forgetting [that it is not required], it does not invalidate his prayer, though he should make a "prostration of forgetfulness." But if one knew of the sound [opinion], then his prayer is rendered invalid [by the prostration]. That is the soundest of two opinions; the second opinion is that the prayer is not invalidated.

If the imam were to prostrate for [verse 24] of Surat Sad (38) believing that it is an emphatically recommended prostration, yet someone following him in [prayer] does not hold this view, the follower should not prostrate with him. Iinstead, he extricates himself altogether or remains standing, waiting for the imam [to complete the prostration].

### *General Conditions for the Prostration*

Prostration occasioned by the recitation of the Quran has the same general ruling as a supererogatory prayer. Its conditions are that one must be cleansed of ritual impurity, free of filth, facing the direction of prayer, and have one's nakedness covered.

### *Various Rulings Related to the Prostration*

1. Bowing does not take the place of prostration for Quranic recitation if the prostration is optional. This is al-Shafi'i's opinion and the opinion of the majority of scholars. Abu Hanifa said that the bowing may take its place. (May Allah grant them His mercy.)

2. If one recites a verse of prostration while riding an animal during a journey, one prostrates by way of gesture. As for someone riding an animal but not traveling, it is not permissible for him to prostrate by way of gesture.

3. If one recites a verse of prostration in Persian, it is our opinion that one does not prostrate. Abu Hanifa (may Allah grant him His mercy) said that one does prostrate.

4. It is not offensive to perform the prostration for recitation during the times when non-obligatory prayer has been prohibited [such as while the sun is rising].

5. One who is listening [to the recitation] may prostrate with the reciter, but is not bound to him and should not intend to be led by him, so he may rise from the prostration before [the reciter does].

6. In our school, it is not offensive for the imam to read a verse of prostration whether the prayer is silent

or audible. Malik said that it is offensive [in both scenarios]. Abu Hanifa said that it is offensive only during silent prayers. (May Allah grant them His mercy.)

7. If one recites a verse of prostration during prayer before reciting Surat al-Fatihah, [i.e., in the opening invocation,] one prostrates. This is a different ruling than if one had recited while bowing or prostrating, since it is not permissible to recite [while in those postures] because standing [in prayer] is the posture of recitation. If one recited a verse of prostration, then descended to prostrate but doubted that one had read Al-Fatihah, one continues with one's prostration for the recitation, returns to standing, and recites Al-Fatihah.

8. The scholars differ concerning limiting oneself to *ayahs* of prostration, which is when one recites one or two *ayahs* and then prostrates. Ibn Mundhir conveyed from al-Sha'bu, al-Hasan al-Basri, Muhammad ibn Sirin, al-Nakha'i, Ahmad, and Ishaq that they disliked this (may Allah grant them His mercy). [He conveyed] from Abu Hanifa, Muhammad ibn al-Hasan, and Abu Thawr (may Allah grant them His mercy) that there is no harm in this, and this conforms to what our [Shafi'i] school dictates.

### *Those Who Should Prostrate*

It is an established prophetic sunnah for someone reciting [a verse of prostration] and who has ritual purity—by way of water or soil (when the latter is allowed)—[to prostrate,] whether the recitation was made during the prayer or outside of it. This [is also true] for someone listening [to the recitation,] and is likewise established for someone who merely heard [the recitation] but was not listening attentively.

Prostration is established for whomever overheard [the recitation] as well as for the attentive listener—whether the reciter was in prayer or outside of it and whether or not he actually prostrated.

Other opinions include: [1] that someone who overheard it does not prostrate to begin with; [2] that one who overheard it or listened to it [attentively] does not prostrate unless the reciter does; and [3] the one who overheard it or listened [attentively] to it does not prostrate if the reciter was praying. But the correct opinion is what preceded [in the previous paragraph].

There is no difference [in the rulings concerning the *ayahs* of prostration] if the reciter is a Muslim, mature, in a state of ritual purity, and male or if [the reciter] is a non-Muslim, prepubescent, in a state of ritual impurity, or a woman.

Another opinion holds that one does not prostrate if the reciter is a non-Muslim, prepubescent, in a state of ritual impurity, or intoxicated. And some of our Shafi'i colleagues (may Allah grant them His mercy) held that one does not prostrate for a woman's recitation. But the correct opinion is what we mentioned previously.

### *The Timing of Prostration*

The scholars have said that one's prostration should occur immediately after reading or hearing the verse containing the prostration. If one delays it and the interval is not long, one may still prostrate. If [the interval] is long, then one has missed the prostration altogether and does not need to make it up, according to the well-known and sound opinion [just as one does not make up the Eclipse Prayer]. Some of our Shafi'i companions (may Allah grant them His mercy) said there is a weak opinion that one should make up [the prostration], as one would make up sunnah prayers that precede or follow the obligatory prayers (according to the soundest opinion).

If the reciter (or listener) is in a state of ritual impurity when the verse of prostration is recited but makes ablution soon thereafter, he should prostrate [as soon as he is ritually pure]. If he delays [ablution] to the point that the interval [between the recitation of the verse and ablution] becomes long, he does not prostrate, according to the sound, well-known opinion. Another opinion holds that one prostrates regardless [of the interval's length].

Custom [*'urf*] is considered for determining whether the [interval] is short or long, according to the preferred opinion.

### *Multiple Prostrations*

If one reads some or all of the *ayahs* of prostration in a single sitting, one prostrates for each of them—and there is no disagreement on this.

If one repeats a single verse of prostration in a single sitting, one should prostrate for each occurrence—and there is also no disagreement on this.

If one repeats the *ayahs* in a single sitting, the following options are considered: First, if one did not prostrate after the initial occurrence, a single prostration suffices for all of them. Second, if one did prostrate after the initial occurrence, there are three opinions: [First,] one should prostrate for each occurrence—and that is the soundest opinion. [Second,] the first prostration suffices for them all. [Third,] if the interval [between occurrences] is long, one prostrates [for each], otherwise the first prostration suffices [for them all].

When one repeats a single verse of prostration during prayer but in different prayer-cycles, it is analogous to repeating theme in different sittings. But if one repeats them in a single prayer-cycle, it is analogous to [repeating them] in a single sitting, and thus has the same three opinions.

### *Prostration in Detail*

#### *Individuals*

When praying individually, one should prostrate after one's own recitation. If one omits the prostration of recitation and bows but then wants to prostrate for the recitation, it is not permissible. And if one does so knowing [that it is not permissible], one's prayer is invalid. If one descends to bow but does not reach the limit of what is customarily considered bowing, it is permissible [to adjust one's posture and] prostrate for the recitation. If one descends for [the] prostration [of prayer] then realizes [that one omitted the prostration of recitation,] and returns to the standing position [to perform the prostration of recitation], it is permissible.

It is not permissible for someone praying individually to prostrate because of someone else's recitation, whether or not the [other] recitation is in a prayer. If one knew this and still prostrated, one's prayer becomes invalid.

*Congregational Prayer*

If one is the imam leading a congregation, then one's legal status is like that of an individual [in regard to the prostration of recitation]. As for the follower of a prayer, if the imam prostrates after his own recitation, it is obligatory for the follower to prostrate with him, and the follower's prayer is invalid if he fails to do so.

If the imam does not prostrate, it is not permissible for the follower to prostrate, and if the follower were to prostrate regardless, his prayer would be nullified. However, [in this case] it is recommended for the follower to prostrate when he finishes his prayer, though this is not emphasized.

If the imam prostrated and the follower was unaware of it until the imam raised his head from the prostration, the follower's [momentary] divergence from the imam is excused but it is not permissible for him to prostrate. But if the follower discovers this while the imam is still in the prostration, it is obligatory for him to prostrate. Yet, if he descends to prostrate and the imam then rises [from his prostration] while the follower is in the process of bending down, the follower should then [adjust his posture and] rise with the imam; it is not permissible for him to prostrate. The ruling is the same for a weak person who bends down [to prostrate] with the imam, but the imam rises before the weak person reaches prostration (because the imam's pace is faster than the follower's). So the weak person must rise back up with the imam and does not prostrate.

It is not permissible for someone following an imam to prostrate because of his own recitation [in a silent prayer] or anyone else's recitation, except the imam's. If he prostrates, his prayer is invalidated. It is offensive for him to recite a [verse containing a] prostration, and it is offensive for him to listen to any recitation other than the imam's.

### *The Description of the Prostration*

Know that the rulings in this section are numerous, though I will hint at their fundamentals and be extremely brief while retaining clarity.

Know that the prostration for Quranic recitation [occurs in one of] two scenarios: outside of or during prayer.

#### *Prostration of Recitation outside of Prayer*

If it is outside of prayer and one wants to prostrate, one does the following: (1) One makes the intention for the prostration of recitation; (2) says the opening "*Allahu akbar,*" and raises one's hands parallel to one's shoulders, just as one does at the beginning of any prayer; (3) one then says a second "*Allahu akbar*" as one moves toward the prostration, but without raising one's hands. Saying

"*Allahu akbar*" a second time is recommended and not a condition [for the prostration's validity].

As for the the opening "*Allahu akbar*," our Shafi'i companions (may Allah grant them His mercy) have three opinions concerning it. (1) It is an integral part [*rukn*], so the prostration is not valid without it, according to the most obvious opinion, which is sound opinion and the opinion of the majority. (2) It is recommended, and if one omits it, the prostration would still be valid. (3) It is not recommended at all.

*While Standing or Sitting*

If one intends to make the prostration of recitation while one is standing, one says the opening "*Allahu akbar*" while standing, and then says "*Allahu akbar*" again while descending for one's actual prostration. If one is sitting, one stands and says the opening "*Allahu akbar*" while standing, and then descends to the prostration, just as if one had been standing to begin with. The first opinion holds that this is recommended. A group of our Shafi'i companions unequivocally held this opinion, include Shaykh Abu Muhammad al-Juwayni, al-Qadi Husayn and his two companions (the authors of *Al-Tatimmah* and *Al-Tahdhib*),[12] and the Imam and masterfully skillful Abu al-Qasim al-Rafi'i (may Allah grant them His mercy). The second opinion is that [standing first] it is not recommended. This is the opinion that Imam al-Haramayn [al-Juwayni] preferred (may Allah grant him His mercy), and it

12. They are, respectively, 'Abd al-Rahman ibn Ma'mun ibn

is what the majority believe since nothing concerning this has been transmitted from the Prophet (may Allah bless him and grant him peace), or from any of the exemplary Righteous Forebearers (may Allah be pleased with them and grant them His mercy). And Allah knows best.

*Etiquette and Manner*

When one prostrates, one should observe the etiquette of prostration concerning the invocations [*tasbih*] one makes. The manner is as follows: (1) One places one's hands on the ground parallel to one's shoulders; (2) places one's fingers together and points them towards the direction of the *qiblah*; (3) takes [one's hands] out of one's sleeves and places them directly onto the prayer surface; (4) spreads one's elbows out from one's sides and raises one's stomach from one's thighs if one is a male (a female or a hermaphrodite does not spread them out); (5) raises one's posterior higher than one's head, firmly placing one's forehead and nose on the prayer surface, and (6) rests one's limbs during the prostration.

As for making invocations, any invocation will do. If one omits the invocations, the prostration is valid but one has neglected its complete form.

The scholars say that one should repeat the same invocations one normally makes in one's prostration during prayer. So one says (three times), "*Subhana rabbi al-a'la*" ["My Lord Most Great is exalted above

---

'Ali and Abu Muhammad al-Husayn ibn Mas'ud al-Baghawi.

all imperfection"], then one may say, "*Allahumma laka sajadtu wa bika amantu wa laka aslamtu, sajada wajhi lilladhi khalaqahu wa ṣawwarahu wa shaqqa sam'ahu wa basarahu bi hawlihi wa quwwatihi, tabaraka Allahu ahsanu al-khaliqin*" ["O Allah, I prostrate myself to You, believe in You, and surrender to You. My face prostrates to Him who created it and gave it form, who opened its hearing and vision by His power and strength. Allah is exalted in perfection, the Best of Creators"].

And one says, "*subbuḥun quddusun rabbu al-mala'ikati wa al-ruh*" ["Most Exalted and Holy, Lord of all angels and souls"]. All of these are supplications that may be said while prostrating during prayer.

And, "*Allahumma uktub li biha 'indika ajran, wa ij'alhh li 'indika dhakhran, wa da' 'anni biha wizran, wa-qbalha minni kama qabalatuha min 'abdika Dawud*" ["O Allah, write for me a reward because of [this prostration] and keep it with You, and remove a sin from me because of it. Accept it from me just as You accepted it from Your servant Dawud (peace be upon him)"].

And, "*Subhana rabbina in kana wa'du rabbina lamaf'ulu*" ["Transcendent is our Lord! Indeed our Lord's promise is ever done!"] (Quran, 17:108).

It is recommended to combine all of these litanies, and to supplicate for whatever one wishes among matters of the hereafter and this life. If one limits oneself to [just] some of them, one achieves the foundation of the invocation. If one were to not make any invocations at all, the prostration will have occurred like the prostration of prayer.

*Raising the Head and Saying the Closing Salutation*

When one finishes saying the invocation and the supplications [in prostration], one raises one's head, saying "*Allahu akbar*." But is it necessary to say [the closing salutation] "*al-salamu 'alaykum*"? There are two well-known opinions recorded from al-Shafi'i: the stronger, according to the majority of our companions (may Allah grant them His mercy), is that indeed [the salutation] is required.

The second opinion is that [the salutation] is not required.

Following the first opinion, does [the prostration for recitation] require the *tashahhud* ["O Allah, send blessings upon Muhammad as you have sent them upon Ibrahim..."]? There are two opinions concerning this. The stronger opinion is that it is not required.

All of the foregoing concern the first situation, which is prostration outside of the prayer.

*Prostration of Recitation During Prayer*

The second situation is a prostration of recitation during the prayer. One does not say "Allahu akbar" [while standing, after reading the verse of prostration]. But it is recommended to say "*Allahu akbar*" while transitioning to the prostration, without raising one's hands. One also says "*Allahu akbar*" upon rising from the prostration. This is the well-known, sound opinion. Another opinion is that one does not say "*Allahu akbar*" when prostrating or rising.

The etiquette concerning the manner of prostration and the invocations uttered is as we have previously mentioned with regard to prostration outside of prayer. However, if the one prostrating is leading others in prayer, he should not lengthen the invocation unless he knows that they prefer it.

When one rises from the prostration, one stands and does not sit briefly [as one normally does after the last prostration between prayer-cycles]. There is no disagreement about this.

When one rises from the prostration [to resume one's recital], one must stand fully erect. When one stands fully upright, it is recommended to recite something [additional from the Quran] and then bow [as one normally does in prayer], though it is permissible if one stands upright and then bows immediately without [an additional] recitation. [This marks the end of the discussion on prostration.]

### *Optimal Times for Recitation*

Know that the best recitation is during prayer. The opinion of al-Shafi'i and others (may Allah grant them His mercy) is that lengthening one's standing [i.e., recitation] during prayer is superior to lengthening one's prostration.

It is best to recite at night, with the last half of the night being better than the first. And reciting between the Sunset and Nightfall Prayers is also beloved. When reciting during the day, the optimal time is after the Morning Prayer.

There is nothing offensive in reciting any time because of something inherent in that time. It has been related that some of the Righteous Forebearers (may

Allah be pleased with them and grant them His mercy) disliked reciting Quran after the Mid-Afternoon Prayer, but this is rejected and baseless.

The especially preferred days [to recite] are Friday, Monday, Thursday, and the Day of 'Arafah. The [preferred] ten [contiguous days] are the last ten of Ramadan and the first ten of Dhu l-Hijjah. The [preferred] month is Ramadan.

***Losing One's Place during the Recitation***

If the reciter becomes tongue-tied [while reciting outside of prayer]—not knowing which verse follows—and needs to asks someone, he should observe the etiquette related to us from 'Abdallah ibn Mas'ud and others from among the Righteous Forebearers (may Allah be pleased with them and grant them His mercy): One does not ask how to read a particular verse. Rather, one reads what comes before it and then asks what comes next.

If someone wishes to quote a verse [in conversation], he may say: "Allah Most High said such-and-such," or "Allah Most High says such-and-such." Neither one is offensive. This is the sound, preferred opinion, which follows the action of the early generations. Mutarrif reported that the second is offensive, but this is insignificant. (May Allah be pleased with them and grant them His mercy.)

***The Etiquette of Completing the Quran***

As previously mentioned, it is preferable to complete one's recitation of the Quran [*khatmah*] at the beginning or end of the day. Ideally, one alternates between the two: one complete recitation cycle ends at the beginning of the day, while the next complete recitation cycle ends at the end of the day.

The Righteous Forebearers (may Allah be pleased with them and grant them His mercy) recommended that the reciter fast on the day of the completion. They also said that the supplication that is made when one completes the Quran is answered, and that Allah's mercy descends at that time. Anas (may Allah be pleased with him) would [gather his family together after completing the Quran and supplicate with them].

[The supplication for completing the Quran] is emphatically recommended and many reports have been transmitted confirming this. One should be persistent in one's supplication. One should ask for important matters, and supplicate much for the well-being of the Muslims, their leadership, and for all others who attend to their affairs. One should supplicate using an all-encompassing supplication, which includes the supplications of the Messenger of Allah (may Allah bless him and grant him peace).

I compiled several short supplications in *Al-Tibyan*.[13]

13. The supplications are collected together in Etiquette with the Quran, pp148–158. They are also available online at the following link: http://fiqhapp.com/supplication-upon-completing-the-quran/.

When one completes one's recitation of the Quran, it is recommended that one begin the next [cycle of recitation] immediately after it. The [righteous among] the early generations (may Allah be pleased with them and grant them His mercy) recommended this due to a hadith mentioning it. And Allah knows best.

# 7

# *The Etiquette of All People with the Quran*

Tamim al-Dari (may Allah be pleased with him) stated, "The Messenger of Allah (may Allah bless him and grant him peace) said, 'Religion is sincerity.' We said, 'To whom?' He said, 'To Allah, His Book, His Messenger, the leaders of the Muslims, and their common folk.'" (Muslim)

The scholars (may Allah grant them His mercy) said that having sincerity regarding the Book of Allah Most High is believing that it is His speech and His revelation; that it does not resemble anything like the words of people; and that people are incapable of producing anything like it. [Sincerity is] extolling its glory while reciting it and giving its recitation its just due by beautifying it, being humble while doing so, and by correctly pronouncing its letters. [Sincerity is] defending it from the misinterpretations of the deviants and from the opposition of the tyrants; believing in everything that it contains; not exceeding its boundaries; and understanding its knowledge and examples. [It is] paying attention to its exhortations; pondering its wonders; acting according to what has unequivocal meaning; submitting to what is open to interpretation; searching out its universal and restricted [rulings]; its abrogating and abrogated [passages]; propagating its sciences; and calling others to them and to all the sincere counsel that we have mentioned.

***What Muslims Must Believe Concerning the Quran***

The Muslims have consensus that it is obligatory to extol the glory of the Mighty Quran without exception, to declare it beyond any imperfection, and to safeguard it. They have consensus that whoever intentionally rejects a single letter over which there is consensus, or intentionally adds a single letter that no one recited, commits an act of disbelief.

Know that anyone who knowingly belittles the Quran, anything from it, or the text itself—such as by throwing it in the trash—or disbelieves something that is explicitly stated, whether a ruling or an account; affirms what it negates, or negates what it affirms while knowing [the opposite to be true] or has doubts about any of the above—is a disbeliever according to the consensus of the Muslims. It is the same if he were to reject the Torah, the Evangel, or the [other] revealed books of Allah.

***Interpreting the Quran***

It is unlawful for someone to interpret the Quran without knowledge or without the qualifications to speak about its meanings. There is consensus on this. It is permissible and fitting that only scholars interpret [the Quran], and there is consensus concerning this as well.

It is unlawful to argue or debate about the Quran without justification, as in the case of a person who realizes that a verse likely runs contrary to his opinion and carries a remote possibility of concurring with it, yet insists on applying it to his opinion and [persists in] debating it, even though it is apparent to him that it runs contrary to his view. (But if this not apparent to him, then he is excused.)

### *Saying "I Was Caused To Forget" Instead of "I Forgot"*

It is offensive to say, "I forgot such-and-such verse." Instead, one should say, "I was caused to forget it" or "I was caused to neglect it."

It is permissible to say, "Surat al-Baqarah," "Surat al-'Imran," "Surat al-Nisa," and the like for all the *surahs*, without there being any offensiveness in [saying "*surah*"]. The hadiths and statements of the Righteous Forebearers concerning this are numerous, though some scholars of the early generations disliked this [choice of words] (may Allah be pleased with them and grant them His mercy). They opined that one should instead say, "The *surah* in which the cow [*al-baqarah*] is mentioned," and so on. The correct opinion is that it is not offensive.

It is not offensive to say, "This is the recitation of Abu 'Amr," or "the recitation of Nafi,"or "...of Hamza," or someone else. Some of the Righteous Forebearers (may Allah be pleased with them and grant them His mercy) disliked this. But the correct opinion is the first, and it conforms to the actions of the early generations.

### *Blowing One's Breath with the Words of the Quran for Protective Purposes*

It is not offensive to "blow one's breath" while reciting Quran for protecting purposes. This "blowing" [*al-nafath*] is a light breath without saliva.

A group of the Righteous Forebearers disliked it, including the Companion Abu Juhayfa, al-Hasan al-Basrii, and Ibrahim al-Nakha'i. (May Allah be pleased with them and grant them His mercy.)

The preferred opinion is the first, since it was established in *Sahih al-Bukhari* and *Sahih Muslim* that the Messenger of Allah (may Allah bless him and grant him peace) did it.

### *The Quran as Decoration*

It is offensive to decorate walls and clothing with the Quran, or to write it on the [walls of the] mosque in the direction of prayer [*qiblah*].

If one were to write the Quran on something edible, like pastry, there would be no harm in eating it.

If one were to write the Quran on wood, it would be offensive to burn it.

[There is a difference of opinion] about writing the Quran in a vessel, washing it, and then giving the water to someone sick to drink: Al-Hasan [al-Basri], Mujahid, Abu Qilaba, and al-Awza'i said there is no harm in it, but al-Nakha'i disliked it. (May Allah be pleased with them and grant them His mercy.)

As for writing the letters of the Quran on an iron pipe, reed, or skin along with something else, it not unlawful, though there is disagreement whether it is offensive.

***The Quran and Non-Muslims***

A non-Muslim should not be prevented from listening to the Quran.

But he is prevented from touching the text of the Quran.

Is he prevented from learning the Quran? Our Shafi'i companions (may Allah grant them His mercy) are of two opinions: It is impermissible if he is not expected to enter Islam. But if he is expected to enter Islam, there are two opinions; the soundest is that it is permissible.

# 8

# *Recommended Times & Circumstances for Recitation*

Know that this topic is vast, and it is impossible to encompass it all because of the sheer number of aspects that have been spoken about it. Nonetheless, we will touch upon much of it while employing concise expressions.

There is much in the normative practice [Sunnah] of the Prophet (may Allah bless him and grant him peace) about paying close attention to reciting the Quran during the month of Ramadan, and more so during its last ten days, with its odd nights being especially emphasized. Also included are the first ten days of [the month of] Dhul-Hijjah, the Day of 'Arafah, Friday, after dawn, and during the night.

One should be especially observant in reciting Surat Ya Sin (36), Surat al-Waqi'a (56), Surat al-Mulk (67), Surat al-Ikhlas (112), Surat al-Falaq (113), Surat al-Nas (114), and Ayat al-Kursi (Quran, 2:255).

It is recommended to recite Surat al-Kahf (18) on Friday during the day and its night. It is also said that it is recommended to recite Surat al-'Imran (3) and Surat Hud (11) on Friday.

After reciting Surat al-Fatihah, one should recite the following *surahs* during the recommended prayer before the Morning Prayer: Surat al-Kafirun (109) in the first prayer-cycle and Surat al-Ikhlaṣ (112) in the second.

During the Friday Prayer, one should read Surat al-Jumu'ah (62) in the first prayer-cycle, and Surat al-Munafiqun (63) in the second. During the Eid Prayer, one should read Surat Qaf (50) and Surat al-Qamr (54). Or, during the Friday and Eid Prayers, one can recite Surat al-A'la (87) in the first prayer-cycle, and Surat al-Ghashiyah (88) in the second. Both practices are rigorously authenticated from the actions of the Messenger of Allah (may Allah bless him and grant him peace).

### *Frequently Reciting Ayat Al-Kursi and the Mu'awidhatayn*

It is recommended to recite Ayat al-Kursi (Quran, 2:255) frequently and in all places, and to recite it each night when one retires to one's bed. It is recommended to recite Surat al-Falaq (113) and Surat al-Nas (114) immediately after each prayer.

When going to sleep, it is recommended to recite Ayat al-Kursi, the end of Al-Baqarah (Quran, 2:284–86), Surat al-Ikhlas, Surat al-Falaq, and Surat al-Nas. If possible, one should also read Surat al-Zumar (39) and Surat Bani Isra'il (17), since it is rigorously authenticated that the Prophet (may Allah bless him and grant him peace) did not sleep until reciting them.

When one wakes from his sleep, it is recommended to recite the closing [*ayahs*] of Surat al-'Imran (3:190–200).

When in the presence of someone who is ill, one should recite Surat al-Fatihah (1), Surat al-Ikhlas (112), Surat al-Falaq (113), and Surat al-Nas (114) while "blowing" into one's hands then wiping them [over the ill person's body].

And it has been established that the Messenger of Allah (may Allah bless him and grant him peace) read Surat Ya Sin (36) in the presence of someone on the brink of death. (Bukhari; Muslim)

Also, al-Sha'bi reported that the Ansar would read Surat al-Baqarah (2) to someone on the brink of death. (May Allah be pleased with them and grant then His mercy.)

# 9

# *Writing the Quran & Respecting Its Written Form*

This chapter is very vast. I mentioned its main points in *Al-Tibyan.*[14] Here, I will summarize them as much as possible while still being clear.

Muslims have consensus that it is obligatory to protect and respect the written text of the Quran [*mushaf*]. If a Muslim places a *mushaf*—Allah Most High is our refuge—in a garbage receptacle, he becomes a disbeliever.

It is unlawful to use the written text of the Quran as a headrest. Indeed, it is unlawful to use any book of knowledge as a headrest.

If someone is presented with a *mushaf*, it is recommended that he stand up.

The scholars agree that it is recommended to write down the Quran in a *mushaf*; to beautify and make clear its writing; and to be precise in its calligraphy, without writing the letters in an elongated or oblique manner.

It is recommended to include the dots [on the letters] and vowelize [the words of the Quran], since this guards against errors and alterations.

14. Ibid., pp110–18.

It is not permissible to write down the Quran using a filthy [writing implement].

It is unlawful to journey to hostile lands with the *mushaf* [in one's possession] if it is feared that it will fall into the enemy's possession.

It is unlawful to sell a *mushaf* to a non-Muslim resident of the Islamic state. Imam al-Shafi'i (may Allah grant him His mercy) has two opinions concerning the validity of the sale: The most sound is that it is invalid; the second is that [the transaction itself] is valid, but [because it is unlawful to sell a *mushaf* to a non-Muslim], the Quran is immediately confiscated and removed from his possession.

Someone insane or a youth who has not reached the age of discernment is forbidden from carrying the *mushaf*, out of fear of violating its sanctity [due to ignorance].

***Ritual Impurity***

It is unlawful for someone in a state of minor ritual impurity to touch or carry the *mushaf*. It is the same whether [one] carries it by its strap or something else, or whether touching the Book itself, the margin, or its cover. It is also unlawful to touch the bag, cover, or box in which the *mushaf* is contained. There is an opinion that these [latter] three are not unlawful, but the former opinion is the sound opinion.

If [*ayah*s of the] Quran are written on a board, the board then assumes the ruling of a *mushaf*, whether the amount written is little or much. It is unlawful to touch the board [when one has minor ritual impurity] even if it is part of a verse written for the sake of study.

Our Shafi'i companions (may Allah grant them His mercy) have two opinions regarding touching the pages of the *mushaf* with a stick (or something like it) when one is in a state of minor or major ritual impurity or menstruating: The soundest opinion is that it is permissible; the second opinion is that it is unlawful.

If one wraps his sleeve over his hand and turns the pages [of the *mushaf*], this is still unlawful without any disagreement. There is an opinion that it is not unlawful, but this opinion is incorrect.

It is unlawful for someone who writes the words of the *mushaf* while in a state of major or minor ritual impurity to actually carry the pages or touch them while writing. If he does not carry them and does not touch them, there are three opinions: (1) Writing is permissible (and this is the soundest opinion); (2) writing is unlawful; and (3) writing is permissible when in the state of minor ritual impurity but unlawful when in the state of major ritual impurity.

### *Touching Books Containing the Quran*

The sound opinion is that it is permissible for someone in a state of minor or major ritual impurity or who is menstruating to touch or carry the following since they are not considered to be a *mushaf*: (1) a book of Islamic law or some other field of knowledge that contains *ayahs* from the Quran; (2) a garment embroidered with Quran; (3) a gold or silver coin which has been engraved with [Quran]; (4) luggage whose contents include a *mushaf*; and (5) a wall, pastry, or bread engraved with it.

There is an opinion that it is unlawful to wear a turban or garment embroidered with Quran, but the correct opinion is that it is permissible.

It is unlawful [while ritually impure] to touch or carry a book of commentary on the Quran if the amount of the actual Quran exceeds that of the commentary itself. If the amount of commentary is greater—which is the majority [of Quranic commentary literature]—there are three opinions concerning this: (1) Touching it is not unlawful, and this is the soundest opinion; (2) touching it is unlawful; and (3) touching it is unlawful if the Quran is written in a distinctive calligraphy—by being thick, red, or the like. But if it is not distinctive, touching it is not unlawful.

A book of hadiths from the Messenger of Allah (may Allah bless him and grant him peace) that contain *ayahs* of the Quran has the same ruling as legal texts containing the same. If they do not contain verse of the Quran, they are permissible to touch—but it is better not to touch [such books] except while in the state of ritual purity.

It is not unlawful to touch or carry something whose recitation has been abrogated, such as, "When a married man or a married woman commits adultery, their punishment shall be stoning as a retribution," or the Torah or Evangel.

### *Touching While Having Inexcusable Filth*

It is unlawful—without disagreement—for someone with ritual purity but who has a spot of filth on his body that is not legally excused, [such as drops of blood,] to bring the *mushaf* into contact with that filth. But it is not unlawful [to bring it in contact with] another part [of his body], according to the sound, well-known opinion.

The opinion that it is unlawful [to touch or carry the *mushaf* in that state] is incorrect.

### *In the Absence of Water or Earth*

If a person [with ritual impurity] does not find water and it is permissible for him to make dry ablution [*tayammum*]—whether his dry ablution was [in preparation] for prayer or something else—it is permissible for him to touch the *mushaf* [afterward]. Someone who finds neither water nor earth [for ablution] may pray in whatever state he is in, but it is not permissible for him to touch the *mushaf*.

If such an individual has a *mushaf* in his possession and does not find someone to give it to for safekeeping and is incapable of making ablution, it is permissible for him to carry the *mushaf* out of necessity [to safeguard it]. Al-Qadi Abu al-Tayyib (may Allah grant him His mercy) said that it is not essential for him to make dry ablution [for the purpose of immediately safekeeping the Quran]. But what he said is questionable, and one should be required to make dry ablution.

If one fears that a *mushaf* will be burned, submerged in water, fall into filth, or land in the hands of a disbeliever, then he may take possession of it out of necessity—even while in a state of ritual impurity,

### *The Guardian's Responsibilities*

Is it obligatory for the teacher and the guardian of a youth who has reached the age of discernment to require him to have ritual purity in order for him to carry the *mushaf* and the study tablet from which he recites? Our Shafi'i companions (may Allah have grant them His mercy) have two well-known opinions: the sounder opinion, in their estimation, is that it is not obligatory.

### *Commercial Transactions*

We Shafi'is do not consider it unlawful to sell or buy the *mushaf*. Some of the Righteous Forebearers considered both offensive, while others consider selling —but not buying it—offensive. Imam al-Shafi'i explicitly stated that it is offensive to sell; some of our colleagues agreed with him, while others said it is not offensive (may Allah be pleased with them and grant them His mercy).

## *Concluding Remarks*

This concludes what we intended from [writing] this short work. I ask Allah Most Generous that it be a lasting, comprehensive, widespread benefit. My sufficiency is Allah and what a great agent is He! Praise is for Allah, Lord of the worlds. May His complete prayers and blessings be upon our master Muhammad, and upon his folk and Companions, until the last day.

# *Bibliography*

al-ʿAsqalānī, Ibn Ḥajar, and Muḥammad ibn Ismāʿīl al-Bukhārī. *Fatḥ al-Bārī bi Sharḥ Ṣaḥīḥ al-Bukhārī.* Edited by Muḥammad Fu'ād ʿAbd al-Bāqī and Muḥibb al-Dīn al-Khaṭīb. 14 vols. Cairo: Maktabat al-Salafiyya, 1390/1970.

al-Bukhārī, Muḥammad ibn Ismāʿīl. *Ṣaḥīḥ al-Bukhārī.* Hadith numbering according to*Fatḥ al-Bārī.*

——. *Al-Adab al-Mufrad.* Edited by Muḥammad Fu'ād ʿAbd al-Bāqī. 3rd edition. Beirut: Dār al-Bashā'ir al-Islāmiyya, 1989.

al-Dārimī, ʿAbdallāh. *Al-Musnad al-Jāmiʿ.* Dār al-Fikr, 1978.

al-Dhahabī, Muḥammad ibn Aḥmad. *Mizān al-Iʿtidāl fī Naqd al-Rijāl.* 4 vols. Reprint. Beirut: Dār al-Maʿrifa, n.d.

——. *Tadhkirat al-Ḥuffāẓ.* 4 vols in 2. Beirut: Dār al-Maʿrifa, n.d. al-Ghazālī, Abū Ḥāmid. Iḥyā' ʿUlūm al-Dīn. 4 vols. Cairo: Lajna Nashr al-Thaqāfa al-Islāmiyya, 1935.

al-Ḥaddād, 'Alawī ibn Aḥmad. *Misbaḥ al-Anām wa Jalā' al-Ṭalam fī Radd Shubh al-Bid'ī al-Najdī Allatī Aḍlla biha al-'Awwām.*Translated as *Refutation Of The Innovator of Najd* by Gibril Fouad Ḥaddād. Damascus: Maktabat al-Aḥbāb, 1422/2002.

al-Ḥākim, Abū 'Abdallāh. *Al-Mustadrak 'alā al-Ṣaḥīḥayn.* 4 vols. Hyderabad, 1334/1916. Reprint (with index vol 5). Beirut: Dār al-Ma'rifa, n.d.

al-Haythami, Ibn Ḥajar. *Majma' al-Zawā'id.*Beirut: Dār al-Kitāb al'Arabī, 1967.

Ibn 'Ābidīn, Muḥammad Amīn. *Radd al-Muḥtār 'alā al-Durr al-Mukhtār.* 5 vols. Bulāq 1272/1855 ce. Reprint. Beirut: Dār Iḥyā' al-Turāth al-'Arabī, 1407/1987.

Ibn Ḥanbal, Aḥmad. *Al-Musnad.* 6 vols. Cairo: Mu'assasa Qurṭuba, n.d. Reprint. Beirut: Dār Iḥyā' al-Turāth al-'Arabī, n.d.

Ibn Mājah, Muḥammad. *Sunan Ibn Mājah.*Edited by Fu'ād 'Abd al-Bāqī. 2 vols. Beirut: Dār al-Fikr, n.d.

al-Kāsānī, Abū Bakr ibn Manṣūr. *Badā'i' al-Ṣanā'i' fī Tartīb al-Sharā'i'.* Edited by 'Adnān Darawīsh. 6 vols. Beirut: Dār Iḥyā' al-Turāth al'Arabī, 1419/1998.

al-Maqdisī, Abū 'Abdallāh Muḥammad ibn Mufliḥ. *Al-Ādābal-Shar'iyya.* Editors: Shu'ayb al-Arna'ūṭ and 'Umar al-Qayyām. 4 vols. 3rd edition. Beirut: Mu'assisa al-Risāla, 1418/1997.

Muḥammad ibn 'Allān, Abū Zakariyyā Yaḥyā ibn Sharaf al-Nawawī. *Al-Futuḥāt al-Rabbāniyya 'alā al-Adhkār al-Nawawīyya.*5 vols. in 3. Reprint. Beirut: Dār al-Iḥyā' li al-Turāth al-'Arabī, n.d.

Muslim ibn al-Ḥajjaj. *Ṣaḥīḥ Muslim.* Edited by Muḥammad Fu'ād 'Abd al-Bāqī. 5 vols. Cairo: Maṭba'a 'īsā al-Bābī al-Ḥalabī 1376/1956. Reprint. Beirut: Dār al-Fikr, 1403/1983.

al-Nasā'ī, Abū 'Abd al-Raḥmān Aḥmad. *Al-Sunan al-Kubrā.* Beirut: Dār Iḥyā' al-Turāth al-'Arabī, n.d.

Nasīf, Manṣūr 'Alī. *Ghāyat al-Ma'mul Sharḥ al-Tāj al-Jāmi' li-l-Uṣūl fī Aḥadīth al-Rasūl.* 5 vols. Reprint [index in 6th vol]. Beirut: Dār Iḥyā' al-Turāth al-'Arabī, 1413/1993.

——. *Irshād Ṭulāb al-Haqā'iq ilā Ma'rifat Sunan Khayr al-Khalā'iq.* Edited by Dr. Nūr al-Dīn 'Itr. 2nd edition. Beirut: Dār al-Bashā'ir al-Islāmiya, 1411/1991.

——. *Al-Tibyān fī Ādāb Ḥamalat al-Qur'ān.* Edited by 'Abd al-Qādir al-Arna'ūṭ. 2nd edition. Damascus: Dār al-Bayan, 1414/1994.

——. *Al-Tibyān fī Ādāb Ḥamalat al-Qur'ān.*Edited by by Bashīr Muḥammad 'Uyūn. Third edition. Damascus: Maktabat Dār al-Bayān, 1421/2000 .

——. *Al-Tibyān fī Ādāb Ḥamalat al-Qur'ān.*Edited by Ghālib Karīm. Damascus, 1422/2001.

———. *Al-Tibyān fī Ādāb Ḥamalat al-Qur'ān.*Edited by Khālid Khādim al-Saruji. Damascus: Dār Ibn al-Qayyim, 1422/2001.

———. *Kitāb al-Tarkhīṣ fī al-Ikrām bi'l-Qiyām li Dhawī al-Faḍwa al-Maziyya min Ahl al-Islām 'alā Jihat al-Birr wa al-Taqwā wa al-Iḥtirām lā 'alā Jihat al-Riyā' wa al-I'ẓām.*Beirut: Dār al-Bashā'ir al-Islāmiyya, 1409/1988.

al-Qārī, 'Alī ibn Sulṭān Muḥammad al-Harawī.*Fatḥ Bāb al-'Ināya bi Sharḥ al-Nuqāya.*Edited by Muḥammad and Haytham Naẓār Tamīm. 3 vols. Beirut: Dār al-Qalam, 1417/1997.

al-Sajistānī, Abū Dāwūd. *Sunan Abī Dāwūd.*Edited by Muḥammad Muḥyī al-Dīn 'Abd al-Ḥamīd. 4 vols. in 2. Beirut: Dār al-Fikr, n.d.

al-Ṣan'ānī, 'Abd al-Razzāq. *Al-Muṣannaf. Edited by Ḥabīb al-Raḥmān al-'Azām.* Beirut: al-Maktab al-Islām, 1403/1983.

al-Shahrastānī, 'Abd al-Karīm. *Kitāb al-Milal wa al-Nihal.* Printed in the margins of Ibn Ḥazm's *Kitāb al-Faṣl fī al-Milal wa al-Ahwa' wa al-Nihal.* 5 vols. in 3. Baghdad: Maktabat al-Muthanna, n.d.

al-Sharbīnī, Muḥammad Khaṭīb. *Mughnī al-Muḥtāj ilā Ma'rifat Ma'ānī Alfāẓ al-Minhāj.*Beirut: Dār al-Fikr: n.d.

Shihāb al-Dīn, Aḥmad ibn 'Alī ibn Ḥajar. *Taqrīb al-Tahdhīb.* Edited by Muḥammad 'Awwāma. Beirut: Dār Ibn Ḥazm, 1420/1999.

Sirāj al-Dīn, ʿAbdallāh. *Tilāwat al-Qurʾān al-Majīd, Faāʾiluhā, Adābuhā, Khaṣāʾiṣuhā.*4th edition. Aleppo: Dār al-Falāḥ, 1418/1997.

al-Shafaqa, Muḥammad Bashīr. *Fiqh al-ʿIbādāt.*3rd edition. Damascus: Dār al-Qalam, 1412/1992.

al-Suyūṭī, Jalāl al-Dīn ʿAbd al-Raḥmān. *Al-Iṭqān fī ʿUlūm al-Qurʾān.* Edited by Muḥammad Abū al-FałIbrāhīm. 4 vols. in 2. Iranian reprint of an Egyptian edition. n.d.

al-Tirmidhī, Abū ʿīsā. *Sunan al-Tirmidhī.* Edited by Muḥammad Fuʾād ʿAbd al-Bāqī. 5 vols. Cairo, n.d. Reprint. Beirut: Dār Iḥyāʾ al-Turāth al-ʿArabī, n.d.

# *Detailed Table of Contents*

*This page left blank*

Also from Islamosaic

*Etiquette with the Quran*

*Infamies of the Soul*

*Hadith Nomenclature Primers*

*Hanbali Acts of Worship*

*Ibn Juzay's Sufic Exegesis*

*Sharḥ Al-Waraqāt*

*Supplement for the Seeker of Certitude The Accessible Conspectus*

*The Encompassing Epistle*

*The Evident Memorandum*

*The Refutation of Those Who Do Not Follow the Four Schools*

*The Ultimate Conspectus*

ISLAMOSAIC

WWW.ISLAMOSAIC.COM

CPSIA information can be obtained
at www.ICGtesting.com
Printed in the USA
LVHW112133310519
619780LV00001B/2/P

9 781944 904135